T0334352

Cambridge Elements ≡

Elements in Public Policy
edited by
M. Ramesh
National University of Singapore (NUS)
Michael Howlett
Simon Fraser University, British Columbia
Xun WU
Hong Kong University of Science and Technology (Guangzhou)
Judith Clifton
University of Cantabria
Eduardo Araral
National University of Singapore (NUS)

POLICY ENTREPRENEURS, CRISES, AND POLICY CHANGE

Evangelia Petridou
Mid Sweden University and NTNU Social Research
Jörgen Sparf
Mid Sweden University and NTNU Social Research
Nikolaos Zahariadis
Rhodes College
Thomas A. Birkland
North Carolina State University

CAMBRIDGE
UNIVERSITY PRESS

Shaftesbury Road, Cambridge CB2 8EA, United Kingdom

One Liberty Plaza, 20th Floor, New York, NY 10006, USA

477 Williamstown Road, Port Melbourne, VIC 3207, Australia

314–321, 3rd Floor, Plot 3, Splendor Forum, Jasola District Centre, New Delhi – 110025, India

103 Penang Road, #05–06/07, Visioncrest Commercial, Singapore 238467

Cambridge University Press is part of Cambridge University Press & Assessment, a department of the University of Cambridge.

We share the University's mission to contribute to society through the pursuit of education, learning and research at the highest international levels of excellence.

www.cambridge.org
Information on this title: www.cambridge.org/9781009565202

DOI: 10.1017/9781009314695

First published 2024

A catalogue record for this publication is available from the British Library

ISBN 978-1-009-56520-2 Hardback
ISBN 978-1-009-31467-1 Paperback
ISSN 2398-4058 (online)
ISSN 2514-3565 (print)

Policy Entrepreneurs, Crises, and Policy Change

Elements in Public Policy

DOI: 10.1017/9781009314695
First published online: December 2024

Evangelia Petridou
Mid Sweden University and NTNU Social Research

Jörgen Sparf
Mid Sweden University and NTNU Social Research

Nikolaos Zahariadis
Rhodes College

Thomas A. Birkland
North Carolina State University

Author for correspondence: Evangelia Petridou, evangelia.petridou@miun.se

Abstract: Increasingly, policymaking takes place while extraordinary events threaten fundamental societal values. During turbulent times, policy entrepreneurs emerge as pivotal figures. They are energetic actors who pursue dynamic change in public policy and, whereas we know much about how they promote innovation and change in normal policymaking, we know less about how they behave in crises, and even less about how different crises influence policy entrepreneurial action. This Element focuses on interaction between policy entrepreneurs and crises. It analyzes policy entrepreneurial action in six case studies – three fast-burning and three creeping crises – to ascertain policy entrepreneurs' strategies and effectiveness during extraordinary events. It proposes crisis policy entrepreneurial strategies, a framework to understand outcomes based on policy entrepreneurial action and type of crisis and suggests avenues for further research on policy entrepreneurs and crises, including implications for crisis managers. This title is also available as Open Access on Cambridge Core.

Keywords: policy entrepreneurs, policy change, fast-burning crises, creeping crises, crisis management

ISBNs: 9781009565202 (HB), 9781009314671 (PB), 9781009314695 (OC)
ISSNs: 2398-4058 (online), 2514-3565 (print)

Contents

1 Policy Entrepreneurs in a Crisis Context

1.1 Introduction

Crises test the resilience of societies, economies, and polities. Whether it is an economic downturn, a major disaster, a public health emergency, or political turmoil, crises often expose vulnerabilities and highlight the need for public policy change. These challenging events force governments, organizations, and individuals to reassess their current practices, approaches, and strategies to respond and recover effectively. As a result, crises serve as catalysts for change, incentivizing decision-makers to reevaluate existing policies, introduce new measures, and implement reforms to address the immediate crisis and prevent similar situations from happening in the future (Nohrstedt and Weible, 2010). The question that emerges is how policy actors, groups, and institutions use crises in their efforts to achieve policy change. In this Element, we investigate specifically how policy entrepreneurs do just that.

While we know much about how policy entrepreneurs attempt to bring about public policy change during normal times, we know relatively little about how they behave during crises. We know crises are, by definition, extraordinary events, so it is logical to expect entrepreneurial action to be equally extraordinary or at least different in strategy or intensity, if not aims. To understand the difference, we examine policy entrepreneurial action during diverse crisis contexts to ascertain the strategies and effectiveness of entrepreneurs in extraordinary circumstances. We argue that despite some similarities, important differences in entrepreneurial approaches and action must be specified and elaborated to gain a better and more nuanced understanding of how and why entrepreneurs bring about policy change during crises. To organize the analysis, we use two factors that contribute to understanding entrepreneurial engagement during crises: entrepreneurial action (proactive vs. reactive) and crisis emergence (fast-burning vs. creeping). We proceed inductively and use the case studies to generate hypotheses and construct a framework, which we flesh out in some theoretical detail in Section 5.

Policy entrepreneurs, these energetic actors who engage in collaborative efforts in and around government to promote policy innovations (Mintrom, 2019a), have long been recognized as agents of policy change (Kingdon, 2011; Mintrom, 2000; Roberts and King, 1991; Schneider and Teske, 1992; Schneider et al., 1995). For this reason, in the past few decades, they have attracted considerable academic attention, enriching scholarship that is constantly evolving (Arnold, 2015, 2021; Cohen, 2021; Cohen et al., 2023; Frisch Aviram et al., 2020; Mintrom, 2019a, b; Mintrom and Norman, 2009; Petridou, 2017; Petridou and Mintrom, 2021). The policy entrepreneur gained purchase in public policy studies with the publication of Kingdon's seminal 1984 book *Agendas, Alternatives, and Public Policies,* where entrepreneurs were defined as "advocates for proposals or for the prominence of ideas" (Kingdon, 2011, p. 122); they are the actors without whom the coupling of the independent policy, politics, and politics streams in the Multiple Streams Framework (MSF) would not be possible. Policy entrepreneurs constitute a distinct kind of political actor (Mintrom, 2019a, b; Petridou and Mintrom, 2021), but they also have other identities in and around government. They may be elected or non-elected officials (Carter and Scott, 2009, 2010; Svensson, 2019), members of civil society or interest groups (Anderson et al., 2019; Verduijn, 2015), or concerned, engaged citizens (Callaghan and Sylvester, 2021).

The arena in which policy entrepreneurial action plays out, the policymaking process, increasingly takes place against the backdrop of one or more unfolding crises. The time available for decision-making is consequentially truncated, and levels of uncertainty are heightened (Boin et al., 2017). The original word, derived from the Greek for "judgment" or "trial," also conveys the notion of critical juncture as a delineation of time and space necessitating complex decision-making under time pressure and an imminent threat in the face of uncertainty and ambiguous choices (Petridou and Sparf, 2017).

Much scholarly attention has been paid to the role of policy entrepreneurs in delivering policy innovation when the right opportunity arises or when the entrepreneurs themselves create the right opportunity. The dual aspect of crisis as a devastating event for those directly affected by it and as an impetus for innovation in the public sector and the market lends itself as a propitious opportunity structure for policy entrepreneurs. For example, David (2015, p. 159) recounts how George W. Bush and Dick Cheney "seized and exploited the opportunities created by the post 9/11 political climate and became the public face of the argument for a firm link between Saddam Hussein and Al-Qaeda, and for evidence of weapons of mass destruction (including nuclear arms) in Iraq" resulting in the American invasion of Iraq in 2003 and the legal redefinition of torture. Similarly, in a very different policy area, national context, and crisis, Nygaard-Christensen and Houborg (2023) demonstrate how the COVID-19 pandemic necessitated – and resulted in – increased coordination among bureaucracies dealing with health care, which in turn was used by policy entrepreneurs to initiate innovation in treatment services geared towards patients with drug addiction. A third example of the interaction between crises and policy entrepreneurship is in Saurugger and Terpan (2016), who show how complex institutional contexts such as the European Union require coherent entrepreneurial coalitions to achieve policy change.

Despite the notion that policy entrepreneurs and crisis events interact, especially in the context of some policy frameworks, for example, the MSF (Herweg et al., 2023; Zahariadis et al., 2023), as we will demonstrate later in this section there have been few systematic attempts to understand the timing, extent, and substance of policy entrepreneurial action in crisis contexts. This Element thus constitutes a theoretically based and empirically supported joint investigation of policy entrepreneurs and crisis interactions. In the remainder of this section, we briefly introduce the concepts of policy entrepreneur, policy entrepreneurship, and crisis, followed by a brief literature review at the intersection of these terms. We conclude with a roadmap for the remaining four sections of the book.

1.2 Defining Policy Entrepreneurs, Policy Entrepreneurship, and Crises

1.2.1 Policy Entrepreneurs and Policy Entrepreneurship

Policy entrepreneurs have been theorized extensively in the policy studies scholarship, and their importance as a heuristic for agency has been recognized not only in theories of the policy process but also as a stand-alone concept (Petridou, 2014). All entrepreneurs in the public sphere perform three functions: they discover unmet needs and select suitable solutions for them; they bear the risk (personal, political, or economic) associated with introducing these solutions, and they build teams of individuals willing to work together towards the realization of the proposed solutions (Schneider and Teske, 1992; Schneider et al., 1995). Additionally, policy entrepreneurs are creative and strategic in that they must be able to think ahead how their proposals may influence the policy debate not only in the short run but also in the long run. These actors are socially competent and able to read cues so that they may anticipate how others will receive their proposed solutions, for which they must be able to argue persuasively in well-maintained and broad networks. Finally, policy entrepreneurs are expected to be competent leaders of the coalitions they assemble (Mintrom, 2000). Necessary requirements for the success of policy entrepreneurial action include (i) telling a persuasive story which frames the problem in a way that is attractive to policymakers, (ii) ensuring the preferred solution is available prior to entrepreneurs drawing attention to a problem, and (iii) exploiting a propitious moment in time, a window of opportunity, during which policymakers are willing to listen in order to realize their policy solution (Cairney, 2018).

Less scholarly attention has been paid to the concept of policy entrepreneurship. This is not necessarily surprising, given that the policy entrepreneur has widely been used as a heuristic for agency, which in turn is often treated as a residual variable explaining change when structural variables fail to do so (Capano and Galanti, 2018). In other words, public policy scholars are interested in the entrepreneur as an actor, not in entrepreneurship as a process. Yet, understanding entrepreneurship can further the understanding of the entrepreneur. We follow Kirzner (1973), who viewed entrepreneurship as a process rather than an end state. We define policy entrepreneurship as the process that enables entrepreneurs to discern the most expedient instance to act in order to achieve their goal of affecting change.

1.2.2 What Is a Crisis?

A crisis is an unusual situation that presents some extraordinary challenges for those directly affected (Almond et al., 1973). Early political science literature drawing from international relations, defined a crisis as:

> a situation where three necessary and sufficient conditions derive from a change in a state's external or internal environment. All three are perceptions held by the highest level of decision-makers of the actor concerned: (1) *a threat to basic values*, along with (2) the awareness of *finite time for response* to the external value threat, and (3) *a high probability of involvement in military hostilities*. (Brecher et al., 1988, p. 3, emphasis in the original)

Even in the contemporary crisis landscape, where threats include a host of non-state actors and implications that are broader than the engagement in military hostilities, the basic tenets of this definition still hold. Moreover, while there are examples of definitions that allude to the idea that crises are not entirely bad – including the notion crises present opportunities (Dror, 1993; Stranks, 1994), that crises contain an element of duality (Drennan et al., 2015) consisting of a historical period of rupture (from the business-as-usual) and a framed event (Gotham and Greenberg, 2014), or that they constitute a turning point or critical juncture (Petridou and Sparf, 2017), the idea of crisis as a predominantly negative situation prevails (Shaluf et al., 2003). Broadly, the term implies an undesirable and unexpected situation that possesses current or latent harm to people, organizations, or society, engendering feelings of panic, fear, danger, or shock (Darling, 1994).

In the crisis management literature, a crisis constitutes "a serious threat to the basic structures or the fundamental values and norms of a system, which under time pressure and highly uncertain circumstances necessitates making vital decisions" (Rosenthal et al., 1989, p. 10). Boin et al. (2017) draw from this definition to conceptualize crises as "critical junctures in the lives of systems – times at which their ability to function can no longer be taken for granted" (Boin et al., 2017, p. 5). Boin et al. (2017) go on to say that during a crisis, a community, organization, region, or country (all of which constitute a system) experiences an urgent threat to the values that they consider fundamental for their existence. This threat necessarily contains a host of unknown contingencies and necessitates urgent action.

The definitions above are not dissimilar to each other in that they all contain the key elements of a crisis: the *threat* it poses to a system, the *time pressure* that crisis managers experience when dealing with a crisis, and the *uncertainty* and the concomitant *ambiguity* regarding both the causes of the crisis and the "best" ways to manage and contain it in a way that limits harm done. The extent of harm done – in other words, the magnitude of the framed-as-crisis-event – depends on the existing landscape of risk and resilience in a given society, which in turn is informed by power differentials and degree of inequality of environmental protections (Gotham and Greenberg, 2014). Failure to successfully manage the crisis raises important questions about the competence of the governing coalition and can bring governments down. The so-called Partygate Scandal in 2020–2021, for example, eventually led to the resignation of UK Prime Minister Boris Johnson and considerable leadership turmoil in the governing party in 2023. In the United States, the poor response to Hurricane Katrina in 2005 led to significant criticism of the Bush administration and greatly weakened its second term.

By definition, the crisis management literature offers guidance regarding how disasters should be managed – that is, how their adverse effects can be prevented, mitigated, or controlled. Successful crisis management is generally good for society because it can guide society away from harm. Still, successful crisis management is often framed in terms of its value to the entity managing the crisis. The historical trajectory of crisis management spans an extensive and intricate timeline characterized by the gradual evolution of strategies and practices employed by civilizations to navigate and mitigate a variety of crisis events. The origins of crisis management can be traced as far back as in ancient civilizations such as the Egyptians, Greeks, and Romans (Rainbird, 1976), and success or failure reflected accordingly on the ruling entity governing the crisis management efforts.

In the contemporary era, crisis management has seen significant advancements in dealing with emerging complexities such as terrorism, cybersecurity vulnerabilities, and pandemics. National and international institutions and private sector organizations have produced comprehensive crisis management plans and strategies. Over time, the field of crisis management has demonstrated a capacity to evolve in response to the dynamic characteristics of crises, resulting in the establishment of more formalized and specialized approaches. Currently, the management of crises encompasses not only governmental entities but also international organizations such as the European Union Emergency Response Coordination Centre (ERCC), which is the heart of the EU Civil Protection Mechanism, non-governmental organizations, and the business sector, fostering collaborative efforts to alleviate, address, and recover from diverse forms of emergencies (Drennan et al., 2015). This is not surprising in an era where the state has essentially declared its inability to keep citizens safe (Evans and Reid, 2014) and calls upon the entire society to contribute to its own resilience and safety.

An important threshold question in this literature concerns the extent to which a crisis is endogenous – that is, an *organizational* crisis brought on by failures, shortcomings, and malevolent behavior in a particular organization – or whether it is an exogenous shock to a political or governance system that should be controlled, but that is not credibly *caused* by the entity seeking to manage the crisis. As Seeger et al. (1998, p. 233) argue, "organizational crises are conceptually distinct from disasters, which are usually defined in the research literature as non-organizationally based events generated by natural or mass technological forces".

This distinction may be naive. Organizations are normatively expected to be prepared to protect people from a dizzying array of financial, technological, and environmental risks (Beck, 1992; Birkland and Nath, 2000; Perrow, 1999). The legitimacy of the responsible organizations or the social, political, and economic system of which these organizations are a part may be eroded if these organizations fail to address a crisis effectively, particularly if the crisis is either caused, somehow, by poor decisions made by an organization or whether, once confronted with a crisis they did not cause, they fail to respond effectively or fail to even imagine that the event could happen. For example, a food poisoning crisis may implicate the supplier of food to a restaurant, the restaurant that prepared the food, and the government organization that regulates food safety. In such a case, while the restaurant may not have caused the food to be tainted, they should have anticipated the *possibility* that food could be unsanitary and should have systems in place to prevent their serving contaminated food, even though the fact that the food was tainted was the fault of a supplier (Birkland and Nath, 2000). The September 11 terror attacks in the United States were a crisis because of the physical harm they did, the increased sensitivity to the possibility of mass-casualty terrorism, *and* the Bush Administration's failure to detect and thwart the plot in the face of a growing realization that terrorism poses a threat to the United States. In the contemporary policy environment characterized by networked governance and in a complex risk environment, efforts to claim that a crisis event is unforeseeable and uncontrollable for which an organization cannot be expected to prepare is, at best, unrealistic. As Darling (1994) notes, successful firms anticipate potential crises and seek to manage risks before they develop into crises. This is true of any organization, including the public sector.

The crisis management literature also implicitly recognizes that labeling an event a crisis is a political act (Boin et al., 2017; Edelman, 1977), as contestants in the policy process engage in framing contests in an effort to elevate or block issues from reaching the agenda. Participants may claim that a current situation – such as the large number of migrants at the Mexico-US border – is a current crisis, or more forward-thinking actors anticipate policy problems before they arise (DeLeo, 2016).

1.2.3 Crises as Focusing Events

Crises can be characterized as *focusing events* or as having been triggered by such an event. A potential focusing event is an event that is "sudden, relatively rare, can be reasonably defined as harmful or revealing the possibility of potentially greater future harms, inflicts harms or suggests potential harms that are or could be concentrated on a definable geographical area or community of interest, and that is known to policymakers and the public virtually simultaneously" (Birkland, 1997, p. 22). We cannot know in advance whether a particular event will be a focusing event; that is, we do not know that the event will have a substantial effect on the political agenda. The logic of MSF suggests that a focusing event is an event that opens up the agenda to new contestants in policy debates, and those contestants – often as policy entrepreneurs – find that the event is an opportunity to couple solutions with problems. Kingdon (2011) identified focusing events as one way in which issues gain greater attention, along with changes in indicators and spillovers from other domains, though he never provided a definition of focusing events as narrowly focused as Birkland. But regardless of how we conceive of focusing events, they typically reach the agenda because they reveal policy failures and may, therefore, trigger policy learning (Birkland, 2006). Disasters create learning opportunities because they create "cognitive openness" to change (Stern, 1997) on the part of actors in the policy subsystem. As Birkland argued, "focusing events can be used to demonstrate the existence of policy failure; that is, participants in policymaking can reasonably argue that a focusing event would not have happened or would not have been so severe 'if only' something had been done" (Birkland, 2004, p. 343).

In MSF, the interaction between the policy entrepreneur and crises is articulated in detail. By coining the term *focusing event*, Kingdon (2011) pointed to the window of opportunity for policy entrepreneurs to link policy prescriptions to the new appreciation of a problem that is revealed by a focusing event. On the other post-event side, the conceptualization has had implications for policy learning. To simplify the conceptualization, we can assume that individuals are the agents of learning. Busenberg (2001, p. 173) defines learning as "a process in which individuals apply new information and ideas to policy decisions." The information need not be new to the policy domain or subsystem – indeed, a great deal might already be known in the problem stream – but the problems revealed by the event may be new to the most important decision-makers within a policy community. Peter May argues specifically that *policy failure* can yield three different kinds of learning: instrumental policy learning, social policy learning, and political learning. In all three types of learning, policy failure – politically and socially defined – provides a stimulus for learning about how to make better policy (May, 1992) and may be used by a policy entrepreneur in their quest for change.

Instrumental policy learning concerns learning about the "viability of policy interventions or implementation designs." This sort of learning centers on policy tools, such as the use of subsidies, sanctions, or incentives. If an event reveals that something about the implementation of an otherwise sound policy has failed, instrumental learning will yield improved policies. For example, after the September 11 attacks in the United States, legislation that removed passenger screening at airports from the private sector to the federal government is a change in the policy tool intended to prevent hijackings. Conversely, social policy learning goes beyond changes to policy instruments and seeks to better understand the problem itself. It can result in a better understanding of the causes of public problems, which can yield "policy redefinition entailing changes in policy goals or scope – e.g., policy direction, target groups, rights bestowed by the policy" (May, 1992, p. 336). These first two types of learning are not likely to lead to innovative policies because they emerge as a result of incremental change.

Finally, a third type of learning is political learning, which is learning about "strategy for advocating a given policy idea or problem," potentially leading to "more sophisticated advocacy of a policy idea or problem." In simplest terms, political learning is manifest when advocates for particular policy prescriptions learn how to make better arguments for adopting those policies. Policy entrepreneurs can be such advocates as they seek to realize dynamic change.

1.3 Policy Entrepreneurs and Crises: Mapping the Literature

The literature on policy entrepreneurs and, to a lesser extent, on policy entrepreneurship has grown considerably during the past four decades (see Faling et al., 2018; Frisch Aviram et al., 2020). However, it aims mainly to understand policy entrepreneurship in normal policymaking contexts in a variety of policy sectors. In this section, we focus on a subset of this literature at the intersection of policy entrepreneur(ship) and crises. In August 2023, we conducted a search on SCOPUS for journal articles (in English) with the search string ["Policy entrepreneur*" AND crisis] in their title, abstract, or keywords, thus capturing policy entrepreneur and policy entrepreneurship. The search yielded seventy-one articles, with the first one having been published in 1990. As illustrated in Figures 1 and 2, the publication trend of peer-reviewed articles combining the terms policy entrepreneur(ship) and crisis follows the publication trend of research on policy

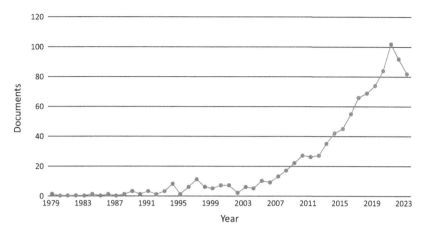

Figure 1 Publication trend for journal articles including "policy entrepreneur*" in Title, Keyword, or Abstract

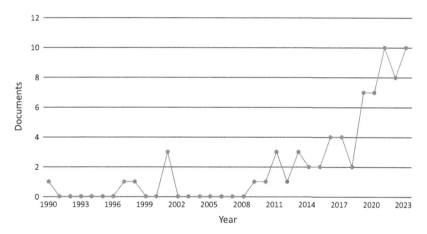

Figure 2 Articles with "Policy entrepreneur*" AND crisis in Title, Keyword, or Abstract

entrepreneur(ship) in the sense that the scholarship has really taken off in the past two decades.

Table 1 demonstrates the distribution of the articles on policy entrepreneurs and policy entrepreneurship and crises across policy journals featuring two or more publications.

In the interest of mapping the literature, we conducted a thematic analysis of the articles produced by the keyword search. The objective of the analysis was to understand the interconnections of policy entrepreneurs (and potentially also policy entrepreneurship) and the crises in which they operate. While a detailed,

Table 1 Journals with two or more publications on "Policy entrepreneur*" AND crisis in Title, Keyword, or Abstract

Journal	Number of articles
Public Administration	4
Journal of European Integration	3
Policy Sciences	3
Policy Studies Journal	3
Politics and Policy	3
Governance	2
Journal of European Public Policy	2
Journal of Public Policy	2
Review of Policy Research	2

systematic analysis was beyond the scope of this section, our goal was to provide broad insights into the connections between policy entrepreneurial and crises. The analysis was primarily inductive, guided by the following broad questions:

- To what degree and in what way do these studies engage policy entrepreneurs with the crises in which they operate?
- Is the policy entrepreneur theorized as part of a theory of the policy process or as a stand-alone cross-cutting concept?
- What is the contribution, if there is one at all, of the insertion of the concept of crisis in the study of policy entrepreneurial action?

Based on these premises, two broad categories of studies emerge: MSF-oriented analyses and studies using the policy entrepreneur as a stand-alone concept. Finally, we found one theoretical piece directly tackling extraordinary policy-making and one article connecting policy entrepreneurial action and compound crises through the lens of the Narrative Policy Framework (NPF).

In MSF analyses, crises provide context; they contribute towards a conceptual shift from the entrepreneur to entrepreneurship (Zahariadis and Exadaktylos, 2016), which, in essence, shifts the focus from the actors themselves to contextual factors that may foster or hinder not only the emergence, but also the success of policy entrepreneurial action. In these studies, crises are extraordinary events that are in the background of the policy processes conceptualized in MSF. The framework, though it accounts for crises as focusing events, does not differentiate between different types of crises and their effects on policymaking in general and policy entrepre-neurial action in particular. In these analyses, the crisis context may constitute economic crises, either directly affecting the national context (Aberbach and

Christensen, 2001; Zahariadis and Exadaktylos, 2016) or increasing the levels of ambiguity at the European Union level (Copeland and James, 2014); the COVID-19 pandemic (Nygaard-Christensen and Houborg, 2023), and foreign policy and the threat of international conflict (Blavoukos and Bourantonis, 2012), to name a few. Dimensions of the crisis, such as its temporal aspects, severity, and impact are largely unproblematized in the policy studies literature.

In contrast, Dolan's (2021) study of extreme weather and climate change adaptation puts crises at the forefront within MSF, at least insofar as they affect the coupling of streams if not necessarily the policy entrepreneurial actions that facilitate this coupling. More specifically, Dolan (2021) differentiates between "sudden, rare, and harmful Birklandian focusing events that can clarify problems and suggest solutions, [and] slow onset issues like drought and climate change, [which] are easy targets for framing contests" (p. 717) resulting in lack of innovation and the adoption of familiar policy solutions. Especially when it comes to climate change, extreme weather events may be interpreted as isolated random occurrences that may be ameliorated by, for example, bureaucratic reorganizations (Petridou et al., 2024). The slow onset crisis caused by big tobacco companies provided time for policy frames to change and thus fundamentally shift what constitutes public good (Spill et al., 2001). Mark Hand and colleagues (2023) also focus on frames and policy narrative but in the context of compound crises – oil boom and bust and the COVID-19 pandemic. They draw parallels between the policy narrator in NPF and the policy entrepreneur, also noted previously by Petridou and Mintrom (2021). A combination of a creeping crisis punctuated by a fast-burning crisis was also used by Vince (2023) to illustrate the power of policy entrepreneurial action in producing a narrative that takes advantage of an urgent crisis – the pandemic – to shift the narrative in another – single-use plastics. Crisis as an opportunity is not a new theme and certainly one clearly articulated in the context of policy entrepreneurs (Bothner et al., 2022; Kolie et al., 2019).

Among the papers that treat policy entrepreneurs as a stand-alone concept, an early study, conducted in the spirit of Graham Allison's *Essence of Decision* (using multiple theories to explain one event before choosing the best fit) tells the story of how an entrepreneur contributed to the unfolding of a political crisis. Dunleavy (1990) uses four different theoretical approaches to explain the Westland affair, a political crisis in 1980s Britain named after a failing company that provided helicopters to British armed forces. The author focused on the political ramifications of attempts to subsidize the company and protect its sensitive defense-related services. The most satisfying explanation was a rare account of policy entrepreneurial failure in the actions of Michael Heseltine, the then Secretary of State for Defense. He is portrayed as a policy entrepreneur anchored in the public choice literature (Petridou, 2017), a utility-maximizing rational actor who puts his own personal gain and career advancement ahead of the public good. The paper is notable for many reasons: it is a rare account of policy entrepreneurial failure, and it shows how the policy entrepreneur contributed to the crisis as opposed to the majority of studies that focus on policy entrepreneurs in the aftermath of a crisis. Most importantly, however, it recognizes what has been mostly absent in the policy entrepreneurship literature, in crises or otherwise: it tackles legitimacy and the possibility that the pursuit of the policy entrepreneur and public good may very well diverge.

Finally, the high levels of complexity, ambiguity, urgency, and uncertainty raise the question of whether we need a new theoretical tool to explain policymaking during extraordinary times. Wenzelburger et al. (2019) argue that crisis policy-making is fundamentally different from the policymaking process during normal times, and they construct a theoretical framework for crisis policymaking. It draws from policy process theories while integrating concepts from institutionalism and partisan theory. Policy entrepreneurs play a prominent role both in agenda-setting and decision-making stages, most notably in the framing of an issue resulting either in its de-politicization and thus incremental change or its hyper-politicization leading to dynamic change. Institutional factors and networks are also important, but entrepreneurs are instrumental in all aspects of crisis policymaking. This, of course, is true during normal policymaking as well. This study is a rare attempt to make explicit connections between policy entrepreneurial action and the extraordinary policy environment engendered by crises. In summary, the results of the literature review provided a benchmark, which, combined with insights from the case studies, contributed to the structure of the framework presented in Section 5.

1.4 Element Focus, Structure, and Roadmap

Policy entrepreneurs have traditionally constituted a useful heuristic to capture those energetic actors inside and around government who seek to promote policy innovations and affect dynamic change in a large number of national contexts, including all levels of governance and non-democracies, and in virtually all policy sectors. At the same time, public governance increasingly means being adept at managing crises (Boin et al., 2017). From a practical standpoint, foregrounding entrepreneurial agency may provide guidance to motivated, engaged practitioners regarding the ways in which they may enhance their chances of affecting change by acting entrepreneurially (Mintrom, 2019b). From a normative perspective, given the grand challenges contemporary societies are facing, including climate change, post-truth politics, and armed conflict – to name a few – the ability to drive change for a better future may result in better policies for the public good.

In this section, we briefly introduced the concepts of policy entrepreneur and policy entrepreneurship and crisis and focused on the interactions between the policy entrepreneur and crises as developed in the scholarship connecting the two concepts. The literature does not directly engage policy entrepreneurs and crises. Very few studies show the effect of policy entrepreneurial action on different kinds of crises and their outcomes. The focus of such studies remains on the creation, development, and manipulation of narratives' making meaning function of the crisis event. Crises are relatively undifferentiated and monolithic and remain in the background of the policy entrepreneurial action. In this Element, we aim to answer the following questions:

- *How do crisis challenges affect policy entrepreneurial strategies, including the degree and timing of the involvement of policy entrepreneurs?*
- *How do policy entrepreneurs shape policy outcomes under extraordinary circumstances?*

We consider both strategic and high-level operative entrepreneurial actions in order to capture different stages of the policy process, including implementation. To provide theoretically informed and empirically based answers to these questions, in Section 2, we develop further the theory of policy entrepreneurship and policy entrepreneurs, as well as their attributes, skills, and strategies. Based on Petridou (2023) and Petridou et al. (2021), we differentiate between policy entrepreneurs who are active opportunity seekers (proactive policy entrepreneurs) and the policy entrepreneurs who act entrepreneurially as a result of external pressures (reactive policy entrepreneurs). Concomitantly, we elaborate on the politics of crisis management, including typologies of crises, to increase the analytical leverage of our argument. Finally, we elaborate on challenges for policy entrepreneurial action in crisis contexts.

As we explain further in Section 2, there exist numerous typologies of crises based on the object that is harmed by the crisis event; its spatial dimension, including ripple effects on societal subsystems and jurisdictions; speed of onset and closure; level of uncertainty; degree of surprise; the origin of its causes (endogenous or exogenous), and the success of managing the crisis event (Boin et al., 2008, 2017, 2020; Drennan et al., 2015; McConnell, 2003). Crises may fit more than one category, depending on the factors under examination and the focus of analysis. This means that researchers must decide on the typology that has the most analytical leverage for the case studies under consideration.

We use the 't Hart and Boin (2001) and Boin et al. (2020) ideal types of crises in a typology based on temporal conditions broadly differentiating between "fast-burning" and "creeping" crises. This is an empirical as well as a theoretical decision. First, this classification has been well developed over the years and is mature and broad enough to fit the analysis of most crisis events, including the ones featured in Sections 3 and 4. Second, this typology has temporal and spatial components, which are both relevant to policy entrepreneurial action in terms of level of governance and policy sector and decision-making, respectively. Finally, Dolan (2021) has used this distinction of crises to analyze policy entrepreneurial action and the coupling of streams fruitfully before us. The case studies in this Element are hypothesis-generating case studies (Levy, 2008). Such research design examines "one or more cases for the purpose of developing more general theoretical propositions, which can be tested through other methods, including large-N studies" (Levy, 2008, p. 5). The cases were selected to cover a broad array of crises and policy entrepreneurs so as to illustrate policy entrepreneurial action in diverse crisis contexts.

Sections 3 and 4 constitute the empirical sections of this Element. In Section 3, we tackle fast-burning crises – these events that fit what most people think of when they think of a crisis, and the events that most crisis research has focused on: sudden, exploding events, with distinct edges, necessitating urgent action (Boin et al., 2020). Section 3 focuses on the 9/11 attacks in 2001; the Indian Ocean tsunami in 2004, and the 2014 forest fire in Sweden. In Section 4, we consider creeping crises. Such a crisis has a "long incubation time" and may keep smoldering long after the acute phase is over, which in effect means that such events are not easy to delineate and declare them closed. We focus on the COVID-19 pandemic in the US, the Greek financial crisis, and the Russian invasion of Ukraine. In both empirical sections, we first outline the broad context of the crisis event; we describe what happened and the actions of policy entrepreneurs. The analysis of the cases is structured based on the following questions:

- *How did crisis challenges affect policy entrepreneurial action?*
- *How did policy entrepreneurs shape policy outcomes in these crises?*

These questions scaffold the ensuing discussion, which informs Section 5. In this final section, to remedy the lacunae in the policy entrepreneurship and crisis management literatures, we first offer an analytical framework to understand how policy entrepreneurs engage in crises and what we may expect from likely policy outcomes. The analytical framework was inductively constructed by the insights emerged from the preceding case studies, based on a nuanced theorization of the policy entrepreneur and a typology of crises. We then proceed by inserting the crisis concept, articulated as fast-burning and creeping, in the theories of the policy process that most directly treat agency and deviations from normal policymaking: MSF, the Advocacy Coalition Framework (ACF), Punctuated Equilibrium Theory (PET), and the NPF.

We conclude the Element by proposing a research agenda for the joint examination of policy entrepreneurs and crises. Beyond calling for a systematic treatment of crisis in the policy entrepreneurship literature, we argue for research examining the legitimacy and the consequences of the politicization of policy entrepreneurs in crises and offering appropriate methods to do so. Finally, Section 5 offers implications for practitioners in the field of crisis management.

2 Business as Unusual? Crises as a Policy Context for Policy Entrepreneurial Action

2.1 Introduction

Crisis management at the strategic level comprises the actions of elite decision-makers (national-level leaders, local-level elected officials, and high-ranking public servants) who are called upon to govern during a crisis and attempt to meet the public's expectations in doing so (Boin et al., 2017). The challenges, failures, successes, and legitimacy of leadership in crises have been studied extensively during the past two decades. Boin et al. (2017, p. 132) note that crisis leadership plays a role in the realization of policy and institutional change because "[s]ome leaders recognize a crisis as an opportunity to instigate major policy change and institutional changes (as will other stakeholders inside and outside of government)." These other stakeholders remain unspecified, as they were beyond the scope of Boin and colleagues, who specifically theorized crisis leadership. Policy entrepreneurs, however, undoubtedly belong to this group of other stakeholders. While we know a lot about leaders during crises, considerably less attention has been directed towards policy entrepreneurs during crises, as illustrated in Section 1 by our literature survey at the intersection of crises and policy entrepreneurs. Conversely, in policy studies and specifically in theories of the policy process, we know a fair amount about policy entrepreneurs but less about leaders and how they are different from entrepreneurs in this context. Section 2 seeks to remedy this.

In the following section, we outline the dynamics of crises and the actors involved in crisis management. We also offer insights into the differences between leaders and policy entrepreneurs before we focus on policy entrepreneurial action. The section concludes with a set of policy entrepreneurial challenges that every policy entrepreneur involved in crisis management must be able to.

2.2 Delineating Crises and the Actors Who Manage Them

2.2.1 Crises from a Policy Perspective

When does a crisis become a crisis? By 2023, the scale of opioid addiction and the casualties and misery it has caused in the US had been declared a crisis.

However, for the preceding three decades, physicians had prescribed such medications in large quantities with seeming abandon, while addiction was framed as an individual character flaw rather than the manifestation of institutional failure that is currently recognized to be. Though crises, from a societal perspective, often refer to disastrous events, such as earthquakes, hurricanes, or wildfires, most crises are more or less socially constructed, some of them completely so (Boin et al., 2017). McConnell (2003, p. 393) goes as far as to say that "[w]hat constitutes a crisis is a matter of judgement" rather than a matter of fact, and that *crisis* is a word ascribed to a particular set of circumstances that are outside the scope of the ordinary. This is in line with 't Hart's (1993) early treatment of the term, defined as "a breakdown of familiar symbolic framework legitimizing the pre-existing sociopolitical order" (p. 39), a definition that leans on an understanding of crisis as a situation of fundamental ambiguity, inducing collective stress and create space for the possibility of de-legitimizing existing ways of doing things ('t Hart, 1993). We adopt a critical realist approach acknowledging that objective facts constitute a component of crises, but the delineation of these events in time and space as crisis events is based on perceptions and sensemaking in the sense that the consequences of these events and the narratives surrounding them include interpretation (Stone, 2002) and to a certain extent are socially constructed (Drennan et al., 2015).

The dual nature of crises rests on the fact that they constitute both opportunities for policy change or organizational reform and real events with adverse consequences for the livelihoods of the people that they affect. This duality is reflected in two perspectives of crisis management, the political and the managerial (Rosenthal and Kouzmin, 1997; 't Hart and Boin, 2001). Thus, studies of crisis management, in essence, may be conducted at two levels of analysis: the strategic/political level and the operational/managerial level. The former refers to the "overall direction of crisis responses and the political process surrounding these responses" (Boin et al., 2017, p. 12), which entails a lot of the social construction of crises mentioned above, while the latter comprises the actions of people "who directly experience and respond to a critical contingency (Boin et al., 2008, p. 7). This Element views crises and their management from a policy angle; this necessarily involves both perspectives. More specifically, the strategic/political perspective corresponds to the decision-making process that results in the adoption of a crisis response, whereas the operational/managerial perspective corresponds to policy implementation. We argue that the partial primacy of perceptions revolving around a real event opens up space for policy entrepreneurial action in both perspectives. And yet, the theorization of policy entrepreneurs in crises, crisis management, and risk management tends to be fuzzy and lacking specificity.

Concomitantly, crises are complex events with varying spatial, temporal, and ontological characteristics, even as they unfold at the strategic/political and operational/managerial levels. To add nuance and richness to our analysis, we consider two types of crises: fast-burning and creeping crises ('t Hart and Boin, 2001) based on the rate of development and the pace of termination of crisis events. In binary terms, crises are differentiated based on whether they are fast-burning or slow-burning. Fast-burning crises constitute what comes to the mind of most people when they think of a crisis – a clearly defined event with sharp edges, such as the 9/11 terrorist attacks (Boin et al., 2020). This type of crisis has been explored in the crisis management literature, but also in public administration (see, e.g., Stillman, 2005). Boin and colleagues argue that slow-burning crises (reconceptualized as creeping crises (see Boin et al., 2020), though under-researched, constitute the type of crisis most often occurring in contemporary societies. Creeping crises have both spatial and temporal dimensions, with ambiguous causes developing over time as a result of transboundary processes, most often overlooked by decision-makers until it is too costly for them to turn a blind eye to them. The authors go on to say that climate change, the COVID-19 pandemic, and the increased refugee flows are some salient examples of creeping crises.

Choosing this broad binary typology of crises lends analytical leverage to the case studies examined in this Element. From a theoretical perspective, inserting policy entrepreneurs in fast-burning crises can provide nuance in the existing literature by yielding insights as to when and how much entrepreneurs are involved in the development of a crisis, what drives them, and what strategies they use. On the other hand, explicitly involving policy entrepreneurs in creeping crises has the potential to increase our understanding of the management of the most relevant crises of our time and the public policies that are introduced (or not introduced) as a result.

Theories of the policy process do not differentiate between extraordinary and normal policymaking. Indicatively, crises are conceptualized as focusing events in the MSF and external shocks in the ACF. Conceptualized this way, crises become a moving part of the theory rather than altering the policymaking process altogether. A recent paper posited that policy theories do not adequately account for the complexity, urgency, ambiguity, and uncertainty characterizing crises. Drawing from theories of the policy process and theories of policy output, Wenzelburger et al. (2019) constructed a framework that models agenda-setting and decision-making during crises, in which policy entrepreneurs feature prominently, though perhaps not differently than in normal policymaking processes. Policy entrepreneurs are crucial in the agenda-setting stage because of their ability to sway public opinion and provide competing frames for the unfolding crisis. Equally, policy entrepreneurs are key to convincing policymakers that their preferred solution is the most suitable one. If the issue behind the crisis is hyper-politicized, then the process leads to dynamic change; if not, the result is incremental policy change (Wenzelburger et al., 2019).

2.2.2 Policy Actors Involved in Crisis Management

The examples above notwithstanding, theories of the policy process are very good at explaining the role of institutions in the policy process but less good at specifying agency in a consistent manner. They are also relatively silent when it comes to specifying the actions of leaders. Capano and Galanti (2018) attribute this deficit to the conflation of leaders and entrepreneurs; indeed, entrepreneurs possess leadership qualities that enable them to build coalitions and provide ideational leadership.

In order to anchor our discussion on policy entrepreneurs from a policy perspective in a crisis context, we must first tease out the differences between them and leaders, who have so far shown to be the most salient actors in the politics of crisis management. Isolating policy entrepreneurs in the landscape of actors involved in the policy process is not always a straightforward exercise. Theories of the policy process, having (mostly) developed independently of each other (see Nowlin, 2011; Petridou, 2014), treat actors inconsistently, comparatively speaking, in terms of focus and substance. For example, brokers are key actors in the ACF; they mitigate conflict and promote policy learning within and across coalitions (Ingold, 2011). In contrast, they are much less developed in the MSF, where most agent actions are performed by policy entrepreneurs in the interest of coupling the policy, politics, and problem streams during windows of opportunity. These actions include brokerage and leadership, rendering brokers and leaders opaque in MSF, which is the one theory of the policy process that most integrates the notion of crises through the concept of focusing events. Conversely, agency in the NPF is conceptualized through policy narrators and policy marketers. Hand et al. (2023) and Petridou and Mintrom (2021) have imagined the policy entrepreneur as the narrator and the policy marketer, respectively.

Entrepreneurship has been defined as "a particular form of leadership" with an emphasis on problem-solving and the synthesis of already existing processes in forming an innovative and effective solution (Ostrom, 2005, p. 1). Entrepreneurs are motivated by benefits, including delivering improved services to their communities and sharing the burden in return for increased benefits, the excitement of innovation, and receiving monetary income as well as respect from their positions as public officials (Mintrom in Ostrom, 2005).

Similarly, Capano and Howlett (2009) consider policy entrepreneurship to be a component of leadership. As Petridou et al. (2015) have pointed out, there have been few conceptual distinctions between the entrepreneur and the leader in the literature (though see Capano and Galanti, 2018, 2021). Having said this, Timmermans et al. (2014) add granularity to entrepreneurship by suggesting that policy entrepreneurs score high in transformational leadership as opposed to transactional leadership. This implies that when it comes to leadership skills, policy entrepreneurs exhibit leadership behaviors described as "visionary, change-oriented and non-conservative" (p. 102). This type of leader, accordingly, is generally more effective under socially stressful situations and crises (Petridou, 2017).

In summary, the utility and function of policy entrepreneurs are fairly well developed (if inconsistently) in theories of the policy process, while the specificity of leaders is less developed in these theories, though theorized considerably in the crisis management literature. Policy entrepreneurs have leadership qualities, but at a fundamental level, leaders govern, and policy entrepreneurs promote policy innovation and change (Capano and Galanti, 2018; see also Petridou, 2017). In the section that follows, we elaborate further on policy entrepreneurs.

2.3 A Deep Dive into Policy Entrepreneurial Action

In an effort to capture and understand who policy entrepreneurs are and what they do, Mintrom (2019b) distilled the attributes, skills, and strategies of this distinct political actor. Attributes are personal traits that may be nurtured, skills are competencies that may be acquired, and strategies constitute what policy entrepreneurs do based on attributes and skills. Policy entrepreneurial skills include ambition; social acuity (understanding the political environment); credibility (being considered to have what it takes to do the job); sociability (the ability to understand how one's suggestions will be accepted by others), and tenacity (being persistent). Skills include strategic thinking; building teams; collecting evidence (to use in successful arguments); making arguments; engaging multiple audiences; negotiating, and networking. Finally, policy entrepreneurial strategies include problem framing; using and expanding networks; working with advocacy coalitions; leading by example and scaling up change processes.

Policy entrepreneurial strategies constitute the most researched element of policy entrepreneurship theory. This perhaps should not come as a surprise given that strategies are observable and lend themselves to analyses aimed at explaining the success or failure of policy entrepreneurial action and, more rarely, to analyses that attempt to predict appropriate or likely employed strategies based on the broader politico-administrative context in which the entrepreneur is embedded. Researchers have attempted to group these strategies so that they provide analytical leverage. In a recent literature review, Frisch Aviram et al. (2020) found that strategies including problem framing, offering solutions, forging partnerships (inter-organizationally and cross-sectorally), and networking in government were mentioned in 70% or more among the 229 articles they examined in that review. In summary, policy entrepreneurs are good at inter alia being strategic, building and maintaining networks, building trust in their teams, and telling persuasive stories. More specifically, policy entrepreneurs always think strategically ahead; they mobilize resources and take calculated risks for future gains. They carefully maintain the networks they have and build new ones so that they optimize control of information flows. Part of these networks become their team, in which they cultivate trust partly by telling persuasive stories. It is important to note that storytelling is dialectic and entrepreneurs nuance their stories depending on the audience they tell them.

Prominent in the preceding discussion is the element of *focused intentionality* (Petridou, 2023; Petridou et al., 2024). Indeed, if policy entrepreneurs are to couple otherwise independent streams during ephemeral, unpredictable, and brief policy windows, they must lie in wait for the opportunity to do so. This implies that entrepreneurs play the long game and that they have clear policy preferences which they seek to advance using a toolbox of strategies elaborated on in the preceding section of this section. This is not an accident; rather, it is a corollary of the disciplinary legacy of the entrepreneur as a heuristic. Recent research has added nuance to the drivers of policy entrepreneurial action and especially to the assumption that policy entrepreneurs are driven solely by the focused, intentional seeking of opportunities. Petridou (2023), Petridou et al. (2024), and Becker et al. (2024) draw from the market literature and argue that political actors may be motivated to act entrepreneurially because of a lack of better alternatives, as opposed to the active seeking of an opportunity to promote their preferred policy solution.

In the market environment, entrepreneurs are credited with developing and introducing, often at considerable personal risk, innovative products and services, catalyzing new forms of economic – but also social – activity (Casson, 1982; Kirzner, 1997). Summarizing the Schumpeterian entrepreneur, Hjorth (2003, p. 2) offers the portrait of "a somewhat mystical individual, driven by the desire to create and the talent to face resistance, who created new resources (or new combinations of existing ones) in order to break an old equilibrium and [make] others adjust to the new established one in the economy" (2003, p. 2). Kirzner (1973, p. 16), however, notes that anyone can become an entrepreneur. Entrepreneurs distinguish themselves from mainstream business owners because they demonstrate creativity and innovation in their intentional efforts and ability to "[perceive] opportunities for entrepreneurial profits." In doing so, entrepreneurs perceive the possibility of gaining profit – to sell something at a higher price than the one at which they can buy it.

The evolution of the market entrepreneurship literature has demonstrated that social interactions are crucial for the realization of opportunity in market entrepreneurship. Entrepreneurship is a team sport; creating a new venture is contingent on "the experience of entrepreneurs, their previous occupation and skills development [...] in the networks of fellow entrepreneurs, family, business connections and event contacts with the government" (Mitra, 2012, p. 114). Notably, weaker economies offer a limited range of economic activity translating into fewer opportunities for increased returns of an innovative product or service, fewer jobs, and a lack of a safety net in the event of unemployment. The only option for survival for some is to be self-employed (Mitra, 2009). This constitutes *entrepreneurship by necessity,* which is a product of push factors (external pressures) and refers to the choice of people to be self-employed because they "cannot find any other suitable work" (Angulo-Guerrero et al., 2017; Reynolds et al., 2002, p. 6). Self-employment is a proxy for entrepreneurship, as used in the Global Entrepreneurship Monitor, GEM. Classic theorization of entrepreneurship captures the intentionality underpinning the search for new profit opportunities in the concept of *entrepreneurship by opportunity.* In summary, opportunity entrepreneurs actively pursue and even create opportunities, often while they are already employed elsewhere. The implication of this is that the potential entrepreneur has a choice. Conversely, entrepreneurship by necessity is often the best "but not necessarily the preferred" option (Reynolds et al., quoted in van der Zwan et al., 2016, p. 274).

Petridou et al. (2024) introduced *reactive policy entrepreneurship,* motivated by necessity, to differentiate it from the mainstream (*proactive*) policy entrepreneurship, which is a result of opportunity structures. "Proactive policy entrepreneurs (policy entrepreneurs by opportunity) decide to assume risks and invest the necessary resources to advocate for the design and/or implementation of a public policy based on intentionality [whereas] reactive policy entrepreneurs (policy entrepreneurs by necessity) decide to assume risks and invest the necessary resources to advocate for the design and/or implementation of a public policy solution as a result of external pressures and often as the best, but not always the preferred choice" (Petridou et al., 2024, p. 76). A crisis and the management it demands may be the external pressures constituting conditions of necessity that contribute to the emergence of a reactive policy entrepreneur.

2.4 Policy Entrepreneurial Challenges in Crisis Contexts

How do policy entrepreneurs behave during crises, and what types of challenges do they face? Do strategies during normal times also apply in extraordinary crisis contexts? Does the type of entrepreneur, proactive or reactive, make a difference in either of the two crisis contexts, fast-burning and creeping? We draw from the leadership in crises and entrepreneurial strategies literatures, not in the least because policy entrepreneurs, as discussed above, possess leadership qualities. We hypothesize that there are many similarities but also differences in the types of expected challenges and responses. In the next section, we elaborate on our expectations.

The most immediate challenge of any crisis is *sensemaking* (Boin et al., 2017). The term was first introduced by Weick (1995) to denote the difficulty of problem framing in crisis conditions. When there is significant environmental turbulence, urgency, and lack of information – elements which by definition constitute a crisis – defining a crisis becomes a highly difficult, subjective task. It consists of detecting and understanding a crisis. For example, when COVID-19 first made its appearance in China in 2019, there was a flurry of activity trying to alert authorities to the potentially catastrophic effects of this "new" disease. For mainly political reasons, the Chinese Communist Party (CCP) decided on inaction for several weeks, in fact persecuting those sounding alarm bells outside government-sanctioned channels (Zahariadis et al., 2021). In other words, in the initial steps of this creeping crisis, policy entrepreneurs found it difficult to define it as a crisis mainly because the CCP feared it might have evolved into a political crisis. The idea of a crisis made no sense because the political authorities temporarily denied its existence, with devastating global consequences. In contrast, we expect entrepreneurs in creeping crises to likely be more resilient and prominent in sensemaking. They have years, perhaps, of trial and error in perfecting their strategies of approaching the right audiences and saying the right things to energize attention. Climate change is a good example. Entrepreneurs still face the challenge of sensemaking, but they will not necessarily be more successful. They will certainly be more proactive in framing crises and the problems stemming from them. The situation resembles very much the conditions of normal policymaking.

The second challenge involves *meaning-making*. Entrepreneurs must draft persuasive stories that mobilize, explain, inspire, and reassure. As Maitlis and Sonenshein (2010, p. 561) categorically assert, "the construction of shared meaning plays a significant role in both crises and change." While leaders must face this challenge, policy entrepreneurs must draft a narrative that links problem and solution into some kind of coherent narrative. Crises, by definition, create insecurity that requires attention and some form of response, if not resolution. The forest fire in Sweden in 2014, as outlined in Section 3, was framed as a problem of resources, coordination, and bureaucratic organization with a focus on dealing with the fire after it occurs, not on prevention. The dominant narrative governing the response and the change after the event was shared by municipal leaders and policy entrepreneurs. Conversely, drawing from the COVID-19 example, policymakers worldwide took public health measures on the advice of their experts, such as Dr. Anthony Fauci in the United States, who acted like policy entrepreneurs. In the spring of, 2020, no one had a clear understanding of what they were up against, but experts had to propose persuase narratives that leaders could "sell" to a weary public. They had to create narratives that promoted trust between political leadership and the public in order to foster compliance to admittedly harsh measures, such as lockdowns, restrictions in economic activities or public gatherings, and the like (Taylor et al., 2023). We do not expect creeping crises to pose different types of challenges to policy entrepreneurs in this area. Whether proactive or reactive, entrepreneurs must still mobilize scarce resources, explain, and reassure.

The third challenge involves the *politics of governance*. In creeping crises, policy entrepreneurs help build coalitions in support of adopting or implementing particular decisions. Working out the details of implementing decisions, sounding out agencies that will be involved in delivering the policy response, and stitching together the various interest groups that will mobilize political support and/or votes are integral parts of normal policymaking and entrepreneurial activity. We do not expect policy entrepreneurs to act any differently in creeping crisis situations. There is time to work on these necessary tasks because creeping crises involve less urgency. However, fast-burning crises give rise to different challenges. The ambiguity inherent in crises, coupled with the sense of urgency, requires leadership and likely makes entrepreneurs less prominent and less effective in this role. Building coalitions in fast-burning crises is obviously very important, but the time required to do so likely fosters agreement at the highest levels. When crises involve foreign policy, such as issues of war (see the case study on the Russia–Ukraine war in Section 4), and political leaders likely act entrepreneurially, we expect many similarities between normal and crisis-induced entrepreneurial challenges and responses. In other cases, there should be differences with political leaders assuming a more prominent role.

The fourth challenge policy entrepreneurs face is *upscaling and coordinating innovation*. As Peter May noted, preparedness and emergency management constitute "polic[ies] without a public" (May, 1991, p. 190). Voters do not pay attention to potential policy problems and risks that may very well be part of the unfolding of a creeping crisis and that may or may not come to a head in some distant future. The policy sector is largely event-driven and reactive. The climate crisis is a very good example of this. We expect that policy entrepreneurs will have to spend more time and effort in mobilizing resources, relational management, and problem framing during a creeping crisis. Most crises are inherently local in the sense that the consequences of crises are felt in local communities that are distant from national legislative bodies. In fast-burning crises, innovation often occurs on the ground, at the local level of governance, as we explain in Section 4 during the Indian Ocean tsunami. The policy entrepreneur, a civil engineer, was able to upscale an innovation in building practices from the local to the national through the various positions he held in the national government and in academe in Sri Lanka. Policy entrepreneurs must also be adept at coordinating horizontal jurisdictions because effective crisis management requires effective coordination rather than working in silos. Though we do not expect that navigating multi-level governance structures is different in substance during crises as opposed to normal times, we expect that the ability to upscale and move laterally is even more important during crises.

3 Policy Entrepreneurs and Policy Outcomes in Fast-Burning Crises

3.1 Introduction

In this section, we examine policy entrepreneurial action in three fast-burning crises, which differ substantially in origins, degree of intentionality, scale, and scope. These include the 9/11 terrorist attacks in the US, the Indian Ocean tsunami in 2004, and the 2014 forest fire in Sweden. Despite their differences, these crises developed fast and constituted discrete events with more-or-less defined beginnings and ends. Whereas the forest fire in Sweden was perhaps a typical example of a fast-burning crisis, the 9/11 attacks and the Indian Ocean tsunami may be characterized as agenda-setting and incomprehensible crises (Brändström et al., 2008), respectively. The politics of crisis termination is complex ('t Hart and Boin, 2001), and making sense of these events requires the examination of both salient actors and institutions in the transition back to normalcy – to the extent that this is possible, or for that matter, desirable. Policy entrepreneurs, however, played important roles in all three cases in steering responses in different directions.

The temporal reach of the aftermath of the 9/11 attacks is extraordinary. We also highlight the potentially substantial spatial reach of crisis events. For this reason, we examine the consequences of the Indian Ocean tsunami in Sri Lanka as well as in Sweden, featuring different kinds of policy entrepreneurs. Finally, it is important to take into account both scale and context. The 2014 forest fire in Sweden might seem trivial in comparison to similar events in Canada, the US, and Southern Europe since the overwhelming majority of the affected area was forest, with a single casualty reported. However, for Sweden, this was an unprecedented event with severe financial loss for the forest owners and far-reaching local and national consequences on the structure of fire and rescue services organizations. The cases are arranged chronologically in the sections that follow.

To facilitate comparison, the cases follow the same template of presentation. We divide each case into three parts and follow the same format for each case. In the first part, we describe the empirical context of the case to set the stage for the parts that follow. In the second part, we provide answers to the question: How do crisis challenges affect policy entrepreneurial strategies? In the third part, we ask: How do policy entrepreneurs shape policy outcomes? This template allows us to gain greater systematic insight into the role entrepreneurs played in responding to crises.

3.2 The 9/11 Terrorist Attacks in the US, 2001

On September 11, 2001, nineteen terrorists hijacked four airliners departing from airports in the United States with the intent of using the aircraft as missiles. Two hit the World Trade Center in New York, one struck the Pentagon, and one crashed in rural Pennsylvania after a passenger struggled for control. The Twin Towers in New York collapsed, causing billions of dollars in damage. This tragic event resulted in nearly 3,000 deaths, hundreds of injuries, and massive property loss. The impact in New York, a global financial hub, had profound economic repercussions worldwide. The budgetary implications were enormous. Federal spending on defense increased by more than 50 percent (from USD354b to USD547b) between fiscal year 2001 (just before the attacks) and 2004. This was the largest increase in federal spending on defense since the Korean War (The National Commission on Terrorist Attacks Upon the United States, 2004).

Many people called the attacks "unimaginable." This was true for most lay people and perhaps for some officials in the Bush administration, but the terrorist threat was not new and had been anticipated. But the scope and scale of the damage done by this event meant that the coordinated September 11 attacks clearly meet Birkland's (1997, p. 22) definition of a focusing event: it was rare, extremely harmful, and the fact of the event itself was known to both the mass public and to elite policymakers simultaneously.

3.2.1 How Do Crisis Challenges Affect Policy Entrepreneurial Strategies?

The September 11 attacks may be an unusual case for policy entrepreneurs because the attacks seemed to strike so suddenly and with such grave effect that it became very clear that *something* would need to change after the attacks. The ability of well-placed, opportunity-seeking policy entrepreneurs to influence the course of policymaking after the attacks was also due to the fact that policy entrepreneurs in the homeland security regime address highly technical "policies without publics"

(May, 1991), which offer limited opportunities for mass mobilization. Instead of inciting widespread action, as seen in environmental disasters, these domains rely on the internal mobilization of individuals with exceptional expertise or legal authority. Baumgartner and Jones (2009) term this "Downsian" mobilization, involving actors within the policy regime responding to the "alarmed discovery" of the crisis (Downs, 1972), rather than a "Schattschneider mobilization" (Schattschneider, 1975) that mobilizes typically unseen actors to seek access to decision-making venues (Pralle, 2003). This is not to say that there was no popular support for taking some sort of action after the terrorist attacks; rather, this means that the substance of the policies to be enacted after the attacks would be shaped by policy entrepreneurs.

According to MSF theorization, policy entrepreneurs draw on existing ideas in the policy stream to match to new appreciations of problems in the problem stream. This implies, as Kingdon posited, that there are seldom entirely novel ideas in these policy domains activated during a crisis. Instead, policy entrepreneurs adapt existing ideas to the newfound awareness of problems. Utilizing preexisting ideas is often a more effective strategy than attempting innovation, as policy windows, even those as momentous as the September 11 attacks, remain open for a brief period. Additionally, focusing events often stimulate attention across multiple policy issues or domains (Lawrence and Birkland, 2004). Despite the initial surge of national unity and determination post-attacks, the window to capitalize on this sentiment was brief. The institutional structures that impede change or significantly alter its course did not undergo fundamental shifts after September 11.

Two of the central policy entrepreneurs in the aftermath of the September 11 case were Attorney General John Ashcroft and Senator Joseph Lieberman of Connecticut. Of the main strategies that are key to policy entrepreneurs' success, the most important was in framing the problem. Policy entrepreneurs pressing for rapid change did not frame the September 11 attacks as crimes, even though federal law defines terrorism and hijacking as serious crimes. Rather, these attacks were framed as threats to the national security of the United States. National security threats are usually met by bold measures to respond to the threats and to prevent a recurrence of an attack. Furthermore, Senator Lieberman and his supporters framed the September 11 attacks as a policy failure that could only be met with creating an agency like the Department of Homeland Security, in the most sweeping change to the organization of American government since the late 1940s.

Policy entrepreneurs were also able to work with advocacy coalitions, although the role of such coalitions was perhaps not as great as it might be in other domains. So much of the post-9/11 reforms were driven by processes internal to government that the policy entrepreneurs were inside operators, seeking to balance the forces inside government that would have a role in the post-attack world. This means that, while the September 11 attacks were framed as a policy failure, the agencies most implicated in this failure – the FBI and the CIA, in particular – were *not* made a part of the new Department of Homeland Security, while agencies such as the Border Patrol or the Federal Emergency Management Agency were swept up into DHS. This is likely due to the much stronger support for administrative autonomy enjoyed by the FBI and CIA compared with other agencies. Policy entrepreneurs therefore had to pick their battles and were willing to accept partial success in the reorganization of government.

In the case of John Ashcroft, his concern was less with the organization of government than it was with the creation of legal authorities that would grant the federal government greater power to pursue terror suspects and their organizations. But these efforts were not novel and were clearly an example of joining new appreciations of problems with existing solutions – the so called "wish list" of criminal justice reforms. Attorney General Ashcroft was thereby able to frame the terrorist attacks in a way that would accomplish long-standing goals that would, to be sure, be useful in the pursuit of terrorists but would also, as it turned out, be even more useful in the more typical sorts of crimes prosecuted at the federal level, such as drug offenses.

3.2.2 How Do Policy Entrepreneurs Shape Policy Outcomes?

Policy responses after the September 11 attacks unfolded in three phases. Initially, measures were taken to address revealed policy deficiencies in legal authorities and aviation security. The second phase involved a debate on government organization in the wake of the attacks, culminating in the establishment of the DHS. The third phase saw the formation of congressional committees and the 9/11 Commission, which issued reports to identify and rectify the lapses that allowed the events to occur, leading to intelligence reforms in the United States.

Attorney General John Ashcroft played a prominent early role as a policy entrepreneur, advocating for substantial changes to law enforcement through the enactment of the "USA Patriot Act" on October 26, 2001. Some viewed this as the Bush Administration's "wish list" for criminal justice and intelligence reform, made possible by leveraging the attacks as a catalyst for change. Ashcroft and supporters, such as Senator Orrin Hatch, contended that the Patriot Act was not merely a wish list but was the realization of ideas previously introduced in Congress, yet stalled for various reasons. Subsequent experience demonstrated that the Patriot Act's provisions were more effective in prosecuting drugs and other crimes than in terrorism detection and prevention (Doherty, 2021). Nevertheless, it serves as a classic example of policy entrepreneurs adapting existing ideas to address new problems within a window of opportunity.

The Aviation and Transportation Security Act (ATSA) was adopted on November 19, 2001, and tackled known deficiencies in the passenger screening system (Birkland, 2004). The stakeholders included airlines responsible for contracting and paying private firms for passenger screening, the Federal Aviation Administration overseeing security, airport operators, and concerned members of Congress. Disagreements over enhanced security measures and who should bear the costs had persisted for years before the attacks. The events of September 11th removed obstacles to federalizing the screening function, leading to the creation of the Transportation Security Administration. The primary opportunity for policy entrepreneurship lies not in shaping the federal role in passenger screening but in promoting various technology solutions like passenger and baggage scanners. Technology companies and defense contractors advocated for the adoption of their products in congressional hearings across different aspects of homeland security (Tierney, 2005).

The Homeland Security Act, a comprehensive overhaul of federal security functions, did not pass as swiftly as the Patriot Act and ATSA due to differing participants in the debate. The immediate push for a cabinet-level Homeland Security department lessened with Tom Ridge's appointment as director of the White House Office of Homeland Security. Initially, the Bush administration resisted creating a cabinet-level DHS, uncertain of the benefits of merging diverse agencies and seeking to avoid Congressional oversight pressure.

However, there was significant Congressional interest in establishing a DHS for organizational purposes, providing the authority and resources necessary for effective coordination. Senator Joseph Lieberman, as chair of the Senate Committee on Governmental Affairs (later the Committee on Homeland Security and Governmental Affairs), emerged as a leader in this endeavor. Political pressure led the Bush administration to signal its intention to create the DHS legislatively by June 2002. Notably, the FBI and CIA, the agencies associated with the September 11 plot, were not included in the DHS. Their bureaucratic autonomy and Congressional influence prevented their integration or substantial mission alteration.

In the rush to act after the attacks, policymakers acted before a formal investigation commission was appointed (Rubin et al., 2003). This lack of a comprehensive review, akin to the one following the attack on Pearl Harbor in 1941, was recognized as a significant gap in understanding the attack. Although initially opposed by the Bush Administration, mounting pressure led to its acquiescence to creating an investigating commission (Birkland, 2009).

The 9/11 Commission, officially known as the National Commission on Terrorist Attacks upon the United States, was established to probe events leading up to and following the attacks. It addressed a broad spectrum of security challenges facing the nation. It anticipated policies promoted after September 11, including the call for a "National Homeland Security Agency" and significant White House reorganization to tackle new-century strategic challenges under a previous commission charged with studying terrorism known as the Hart-Rudman commission, which called for the creation of a homeland security agency before the 9/11 attacks (Ellis, 2004). Co-chairs Senators Gary Hart and Warren Rudman publicly discussed their work during and after the 9/11 commission's tenure. It is noteworthy that former Representative Lee Hamilton, a member of the Hart-Rudman Commission, later co-chaired the 9/11 Commission.

Compared to the Hart-Rudman and Gilmore commissions preceding it, the 9/11 Commission very actively sought to promote its work. Its meetings were prominently publicized, addressing a wide spectrum of issues from emergency responses to intelligence lapses. Its scrutiny of intelligence failures significantly shaped the establishment of the Office of the Director of National Intelligence (ODNI), headed by the Director of National Intelligence. This role was meant to centralize intelligence information from various civilian and military sources, though its full potential has not been realized.

After the 9/11 Commission's official mandate ended in August 2004, the members of the commission launched the Public Discourse Project; the commissioners served as its board. Its main aim was to publicly advocate for the implementation of its recommendations. Operating for about two years on private donations, they held discussions on "The Unfinished Agenda" in the summer of 2005. They also issued "report cards" on the implementation of recommendations. Members testified before Congress, gaining more visibility than usual unique commitment to ensuring their report was broadly considered sets them apart as a significant example of policy entrepreneurship.

Think tanks were also prominent in the post-attack debate. The RAND corporation, in particular, had close ties to the defense and security establishment and conducted research and provided policy recommendations on issues related to national security, counterterrorism, and foreign policy. Numerous academics appeared in congressional hearings and other forums, but their influence was not widespread and was variable, so relatively few academics stood out as policy entrepreneurs.

The victims of the September 11 attacks held significant moral authority. An external interest group, the Family Steering Committee, gained attention, co-founded by the daughter of a passenger on one of the hijacked planes. This group pressured the Bush Administration to establish the 9/11 Commission, which was done with reluctance. They also lobbied Speaker of the House Dennis Hastert to extend the commission's final report deadline (Jost, 2011). While the victims' groups had limited influence, they strategically applied pressure to address the failures that led to the 9/11 attacks. In this way, they occasionally served as policy entrepreneurs.

Finally, traditional interest groups were relatively absent from the debates that followed the September 11 attacks, and when they were active, they were generally on the defensive. Civil liberties groups were particularly troubled by the changes to the criminal and domestic surveillance laws. But in the early days after the September 11 attacks, their concerns were often downplayed, although once the passions of the immediate aftermath of the attacks cooled, their voices became more influential.

3.3 The Indian Ocean Tsunami, 2004

On December 26, 2004, at 7:59 local time, an earthquake of a magnitude of at least 9 M_w hit about 160 km off the coast of Sumatra. The ensuing tsunami had tragic consequences; it is estimated to have caused upwards of 230,000 deaths (some estimates put the number of casualties at 250,000), the displacement of about 1.6 m people and economic losses of about USD1.4b (SOU, 2005; UNESCO, 2019). This was the most catastrophic tsunami in modern history, severely affecting coastal areas in ten countries – Indonesia, Sri Lanka, India, Thailand, Malaysia, Myanmar, the Maldives, the Seychelles, Somalia, and Tanzania. Tsunami waves ranging from runups of 30 m (Indonesia) to 15 m (Sri Lanka) to 4 to 9 m (Somalia) and the associated debris devastated coastal communities reducing them to piles of mud and sediment. From an environmental perspective, the force of the waves was such that it caused substantial soil erosion, changed the geomorphology of the Indian Ocean coastlines, and caused extensive destruction in coral reefs (UNESCO, 2019). Indonesia, which is susceptible to such events, was hit the hardest due to its proximity to the epicenter of the earthquake, whereas Sri Lanka had not been affected by a tsunami before – or since. The government of Sri Lanka reported 36,000 dead (the highest number of casualties caused by a natural hazard in modern history [Sakalasuriya et al., 2020, see also Jayasuriya et al., 2006]) and 21,000 injured immediately after the tsunami hit, while in the long term between 450,000 and 500,000 were displaced. Nearly 100,000 houses and 200 educational facilities were destroyed or damaged (Blaikie, 2009).

The area affected by the tsunami is a popular travel destination for Scandinavians in general and Swedish tourists in particular, especially during the holiday season. An estimated 30,000 Swedish citizens were vacationing in countries afflicted by the tsunami, most of them in Thailand as well as Sri

Lanka. As of November 2005, 525 Swedish citizens had been confirmed dead, with an additional 18 missing. This resulted in the tsunami disaster, caused by waves occurring almost 10,000 km away, to cause severe political ripple effects in Sweden as part of an unfolding political crisis (Brändström et al., 2008; Hansén, 2005). Indeed, this was the worst crisis in Sweden in modern times (Hansén, 2005). In the sections that follow, we examine the crises in both Sri Lanka and Sweden; the former was characterized by the direct consequences of the tsunami, while the latter morphed into a political crisis.

3.3.1 Sri Lanka

The tragic consequences of the tsunami in Sri Lanka unfolded in the shadow of the civil war, which has been going on, with the exception of brief periods of ceasefire, since the early 1980s. This is important because the war has deepened existing cleavages along ethnic lines and has revealed new socioeconomic asymmetries among populations, resulting in the creation of new vulnerabilities (Blaikie, 2009). In addition to the large-scale loss of life and environmental degradation that Sri Lanka suffered, the tsunami touched many aspects of society. Most affected sectors include the social sector, specifically housing and private sector assets, as well as sectors that directly affect the prosperity of coastal communities, including fisheries, agriculture, tourism, and transportation (Birkmann et al., 2010). Following the tsunami, international efforts focused on establishing an integrated early warning system for coastal areas in the Indian Ocean. The Indian Ocean Tsunami Warning and Mitigation System (IOTWMS) is an international institution that became fully operational in 2013. The twenty-eight member state group aims to promote communication, exchange of information, and tsunami research, monitor seismic and other activity that may result in a tsunami, and ensure that a tsunami early warning system is always up and running (UNESCO, 2019).

The disaster attracted international attention and concomitant reconstruction funds to the area. Birkmann et al. (2010) estimate that Sri Lanka received approximately USD4b in aid, though the reconstruction was hampered by governance deficits, including centralized decision-making, an absence of a set of standard operating procedures for all stakeholders, lack of capacity coordination, lack of know-how and lack of action, lack of trust, negligence and indifference, lack of feedback from training and simulation exercises, high turnout of appointed officers and over politicization on transfers and appointments of public servants (Sakalasuriya et al., 2020).

Three formal policy changes occurred against this broad governance background: the establishment of a buffer zone and resettlement; the development of

tsunami early warning systems, and the creation of new bureaucratic organizations – the Task Force for Rescue and Relief, the Task Force for Law and Order
and Logistics, and the Task Force to Rebuild the Nation. Implementation of the
establishment of the buffer zone and the relocation of people at risk was less
than straightforward: conflict, lack of transparency, and unequal treatment of
populations, even as relocation offered relief from chronic poverty for some
families, stymied the process. The governance deficits identified by
Sakalasuriya et al. (2020) led to difficulties in the implementation of the
remaining two formal solutions. Here we follow Meydani (2015), who argued
that a low level of governability (or non-governability) and a low level of liberal
political culture among citizens result in the primacy of short-term consider-
ations among possible policy entrepreneurs in government as well as politicians
as the latter seek to maximize their own political capital. "Non-governability"
refers to the lack of institutional and administrative capacity to make consistent
and stable public policy (Meydani, 2015) resulting from a lack of political
legitimacy and a concomitant lack of inclusion of societal stakeholders in the
decision-making process. The lack of inclusion of societal stakeholders,
coupled with a political culture that is outcome-oriented, leads to calls for short-
term solutions (Meydani, 2015). The formal changes in Sri Lanka were long-
term, and though enacted into public policy partly due to the influx of foreign
aid, their implementation has been largely ineffective. This is mainly due to the
non-governmentality characterizing the Sri Lankan political context.

Birkmann et al. (2010) outline a number of informal changes as a result of the
tsunami disaster. We elaborate on an informal change initiated by a policy
entrepreneur focused on the publication of a new set of guidelines for reconstruction (Dias et al., 2006). Ranjith Dissanayake,[1] a civil engineer, faculty
member at the University of Peradeniya, market entrepreneur, and later high-
level civil servant, has had a long-standing interest in disaster risk reduction
efforts in Sri Lanka, especially as they relate to the built environment. A survey
of the damaged structures revealed that changes in construction guidelines were
necessary to build more robust structures that would be less vulnerable to
tsunami events. Houses built on stilts and religious structures, for example,
performed better because they were built adhering to traditional practices and,
in the case of religious structures, stronger. Additionally, Dissanayake pushed
for the consistent and uniform training of construction workers, who had been
generally treated as unskilled labor and were characterized by high turnover.

---

[1] Dissanayake was interviewed for this Element and has given his consent to be named as an
entrepreneur. He is part of the European Commission Erasmus+ funded project *Strengthening
University-Enterprise Collaboration for Resilient Communities in Asia (SECRA)*, agreement
number 619022-EPP-1-2020-1-SE-EPPKA2-CBHE-JP.

How Do Crisis Challenges Affect Policy Entrepreneurial Strategies?

The strategies employed by policy entrepreneurs in Sri Lanka reflect the low level of administrative capacity in the Sri Lankan national context. This entrepreneur was at the intersection of a market entrepreneur (he owns several companies), an expert (as a faculty member of a university and a civil engineer), as well as a civil servant through his position at the university and other governmental posts. He mobilized resources by co-authoring a paper (Dias et al., 2006) but mostly through using and expanding his networks in all aspects of the field of disaster risk reduction in Sri Lanka. Where large-scale change efforts, such as the relocation of large numbers of people to create a buffer zone, may be hampered by lack of transparency, lack of governmental capacity, lack of know-how, and unequal treatment of people, a smaller scale, less formal innovation may go a long way toward addressing real needs, especially if championed by a well-networked expert.

How Do Policy Entrepreneurs Shape Policy Outcomes?

Sri Lanka has not been hit by another tsunami since the catastrophic one in 2004. However, for Dissanayake, disaster risk reduction is a matter (at least partly) of sustainable building practices. His influence rested on occupying positions in the private and public sectors as well as being an expert. By doing that, he maximized the ownership of decision-making resources (McCaffrey and Salerno, 2011) and had a better chance of promoting sustainable building practices in the construction sector in Sri Lanka, a goal that reached beyond the tsunami reconstruction and into the future of construction in the area. Furthermore, in a national context that is characterized by a bureaucracy with low administrative capacity, the agility of a credible policy entrepreneur making persuasive arguments based on expert knowledge and upscaling technical innovation may prove very effective.

3.3.2 Sweden

The tsunami presented an unprecedented challenge for the Swedish authorities, which lacked any kind of coordinating office for serious crises at that time. The unusual autonomy of Swedish public agencies, rooted in its constitution, partly accounts for the lack of such a coordinating body. More specifically, Sweden's government – the ministries and the Prime Minister's office comprising the Government Offices – is small. The day-to-day provision of public services and, to a certain extent, the formation of policy beyond broad governmental guidelines are carried out by a large number of autonomous agencies. What is more, Sweden is characterized by the absence of ministerial rule. This means that even though public agencies are placed under a ministry, these agencies and the public servants who work for them have considerable leeway (Larsson and Bäck, 2008; Petridou, 2020). This autonomy extends horizontally as well: the Swedish administrative system does not allow for one agency to have operative or strategic power over another. In a 2003 essay, the then Director General of the Swedish Emergency Management Agency explored the question of who is in charge during crises in peacetime in Sweden. She concluded that one coordinating agency would be unconstitutional and instead focus on the need for coordination at the operative level (Eksborg, 2003). This means that coordination, especially during crisis events, is an activity that must be fostered continuously with network-like mechanisms across departments and agencies.

Such coordination and the ability to upscale proved easier said than done in December 2004. Since this tsunami crisis unfolded abroad, managing it was in the purview of the local consulate offices. However, these offices were not equipped to deal with the enormity of the disaster and the sheer number of people in need of assistance. The Ministry for Foreign Affairs' response was slow and underwhelming, resulting in thousands of Swedish citizens being stranded without any support from their government or any way to reach the Swedish authorities by phone or otherwise. The fact that the tsunami took place on a public holiday in Sweden when civil servants were off work certainly did not help matters. The failure of the Swedish government to take care of its citizens in their time of need resulted in a decline in the trust citizens place in their leaders, normally quite high in Nordic countries. Characteristically for the Swedish policymaking process, a commission of inquiry was set up in January 2005, named the "Disaster Commission." Its main assignment was to assess the efforts of the Swedish national public agencies to assist the Swedish citizens in Southeast Asia affected by the tsunami. The Disaster Commission found that (i) the Government Offices lacked a coordination structure to handle serious crises, (ii) the preparedness of disaster medicine was insufficient, (iii) the consular management was slow in relation to the unfolding of the crisis, and that (iv) cross-country collaboration could have been better (SOU, 2005).

The Social Democratic coalition government in power at the time had been unwilling to establish a crisis coordination office in the Government Offices in the proximity of the Prime Minister's office. The solution offered after the findings of the disaster commission was a token coordination office called the "*Unit for Preparedness and Analysis*" without any real power. The office had no access to the political leadership and was not part of any security briefing – it was seen as a purely symbolic and "empty" solution (Petridou and Sparf, 2017).

The Social Democratic coalition government lost the subsequent election in 2006 to the center-right Alliance, which ran on a platform of safety and security issues. One of the first things the new government did was establish a Crisis

Secretariat under the Prime Minister's office after the completion of yet another commission of inquiry (Petridou and Sparf, 2017). Given the preceding discussion, the politics of establishing any form of coordinating entity was precarious, to say the least. The new coordinating office was established with the full support of the newly elected government. However, in order for the Crisis Secretariat to be effective, it needed to be adept at managing the existing power differentials in place inside the Government Offices. In other words, for the Crisis Secretariat to coordinate, it needed access to information that the ministries in the Government Offices had and ensure that they (the ministries) were willing to share it.

How Do Crisis Challenges Affect Policy Entrepreneurial Strategies?

Policy entrepreneurs, in this case, were part of the implementation of a reform after crisis, and the strategies are conditioned by the stage of the policy process (implementation) and their other identity (civil servant). Petridou and Sparf (2017) report that the policy entrepreneurs were three actors with a long history in Swedish crisis management; they were credible and perceived as competent, neutral public servants with solid networks in and around government. They were socially acute so that they would intuit the way to navigate the political difficulties inside the Government Offices and bolster the legitimacy of the Crisis Secretariat while solidifying its prominent place under the Prime Minister's Office (as opposed to it being subordinate to a lesser ministry). Petridou and Sparf (2017) report the entrepreneurs being responsive listeners and supporting the needs of the various ministries – using "motivational framing" to provide other actors with "compelling reasons" as to why the new coordinating office is necessary and not threatening (Battilana et al., 2009). Moreover, the entrepreneurs framed their actions in crises that occurred as successes, advertising that the office is a competent coordinator. Finally, the entrepreneurs used and expanded their networks, which were substantial and dense, to mobilize political support. They were able to "pick up the phone" (in other words, working with advocacy coalitions) and directly reach policymakers if they needed to. These high-level public servants were insiders (Mintrom, 2000) in the crisis management policy sector, and relational management was the most effective strategy.

How Do Policy Entrepreneurs Shape Policy Outcomes?

The strategies of the policy entrepreneurs contributed to the establishment of the Secretariat and shored up its legitimacy. Almost two decades later, the office still provides coordination, intelligence, and support to the ministries ahead of and during crisis events. This, however, did not stop the Social Democratic coalition government from moving the office to the Ministry of Justice when they came to power in 2014, thus signaling a downgrade in status.

3.4 The Forest Fire in Sweden, 2014

Climate change consequences have been manifested more precipitously in Arctic and Subarctic regions during the past few decades (IPCC, 2023); however, given the climate of these regions, only recently have previously unheard-of extreme weather events evolved into fast-burning crises. The forest fire in Sweden in 2014 constitutes an example of just such an occurrence. Unlike Southern European countries, such as Greece, which have been plagued by forest fires for years, often resulting in many casualties, large-scale forest fires have not traditionally been a feature of the Swedish crisis landscape. The 2014 forest fire in the Swedish county of Västmanland was the most extensive in modern times. For Swedish standards, the consequences of the Västmanland forest fire were dramatic: the fire destroyed approximately $140 \, km^2$ hectares of forest and 25 structures and resulted in the death of one person. Over 1,000 people and 1,700 livestock were evacuated, while the cost of the damages was estimated at approximately SEK1b (MSB, 2016; SOU, 2018). Containing the fire involved actors from 69 emergency services organizations working around the clock for weeks. National agencies, including the Swedish Civil Contingencies Agency, the Swedish Transport Administration, and the Swedish Armed Forces, as well as a host of volunteer organizations, were also involved in this effort. The fire led Sweden to activate, for the first time, the European Commission's Emergency Response Coordination Centre, actively supporting the effort with aircraft from Italy, France, and Spain (MSB, 2016). This was quite a reversal of roles for Sweden, which traditionally is the country dispatching help rather than being on the receiving end of assistance.

Crisis management and the organization of fire and rescue services in Sweden rests with the 290 municipalities that face the challenge of adapting their crisis management and preparedness architecture in order to be able to upscale quickly and combat the risk (and occurrence) of large forest fires. There is substantial variation in geography, demographics, resource availability, and capacity to manage risk among Swedish municipalities spanning the approximately 1,600 km length of the country from north to south. For example, it is not uncommon in sparsely populated areas for fire and rescue services to be staffed by part-time firefighters. Local government enjoys considerable autonomy, encapsulated in the idea of "local self-government," articulated in the Swedish constitution.

Evaluations of the crisis management apparatus during the 2014 fire concluded that there was a lack of capacity and preparedness at the municipal level to handle events of such magnitude. They pointed to the need for more coordination and increased systematic collaboration, both horizontally across municipalities and across regions, and vertically, between the local and regional levels in the more general spirit towards systemic improvement and change (SOU, 2019).

In the text that follows, we draw heavily from Petridou et al. (2024) and focus this case study on the municipality of Sala, which was affected heavily by the fire in 2014. This case study highlights four factors that created the scope conditions informing the actions of the policy entrepreneur: the focal power of the focusing event, the one dominant problem frame, the convergent policy community, and the other identity of the policy entrepreneur.

The scope of the fire exposed the inability of the municipal fire services to handle events of such magnitude. It created the impetus, and indeed the imperative, for change. The damage inflicted was existential for the municipal fire and rescue services: a fire of this magnitude had never been seen before, and it came as a shock to the entire nation, which realized that such previously unimagined and unimaginable events could happen even in Sweden. The actors involved in municipal crisis management as the fire rescue services organization shared one dominant frame that is, they considered the fire to be a problem of organization and coordination, resources, and timing.

In addition to a shared sensemaking of the crisis, the municipal policy actors had a similar understanding of the forest and forest fire risk, focusing on the safety of the public and the firefighters, as well as safeguarding the forest as a resource (see Petridou et al., 2024). Finally, the other identity (Petridou and Mintrom, 2021) of the policy entrepreneur was a public servant. Traditionally, bureaucrats are policy implementers; however, as mentioned elsewhere in this section, high-level public servants in Sweden have the ability to make public policy due to the high autonomy of national public agencies and municipalities.

How Do Crisis Challenges Affect Policy Entrepreneurial Strategies?

The combination of the factors above and especially the extraordinary focal power of the focusing event created conditions of necessity as opposed to an opportunity structure (see Section 2), resulting in reactive policy entrepreneurship. This forced the reluctant policy entrepreneur to make the best, but not necessarily preferred, choice in pursuing the reorganization of the fire and rescue services. The emerging (reactive) policy entrepreneur, the then director of the fire and rescue services, championed the solution of reorganizing the fire and rescue services. The policy entrepreneur had no prior intentions to reform his organization. He acted entrepreneurially only after the 2014 fire, which compelled him to act because he felt he had no other choice. He tapped into his considerable networks and discovered an existing solution: to transition from a stand-alone municipal organization to one that was part of a large association of fire and rescue services based in Stockholm. The main strategy the policy entrepreneur deployed in this case was using and expanding his network. The depoliticized frame of the forest fire as an organizational issue did not necessitate intense efforts to convince local politicians of the merits of the policy solution. Unlike policy entrepreneurs who seek opportunities and use their networks to mobilize resources, this policy entrepreneur used his network for knowledge and information sharing and to boost legitimacy in a quest for a solution to a vexing problem.

How Do Policy Entrepreneurs Shape Policy Outcomes?

This policy entrepreneur was a public servant in a position of authority, with considerable freedom when it came to the implementation of directives from local politicians. He was also operating under time constraints, and the objective was to find a satisfactory solution to what was framed as a technical-administrative problem by a convergent policy community. Such conditions (a [reactive] policy entrepreneur, the aftermath of a crisis, local public administration) left little room for creative experimentation, leading to uncertain results. Instead, the reactive policy entrepreneur favored a pre-existing, tested solution – one that was ultimately legislated at the national level and is currently the norm for fire and rescue services in Sweden (see Eriksson et al., 2023).

3.5 Conclusions: Fast-Burning Crises and Public Policy Change

Sudden, fast crises often provide space for policy change. Policy entrepreneurial action in the 9/11 attacks and the Indian Ocean tsunami involved opportunity-seeking, proactive entrepreneurs, whereas the forest fire in Sweden entailed a reactive policy entrepreneur. Policy change (even the relatively common organization reform) would not have happened had it not been for the occurrence of the crisis. Having said this, policy entrepreneurial action may or may not be different in substance during fast-burning crises; however, the high levels of urgency and uncertainty accelerate and intensify entrepreneurial strategies – and potentially increase the impact of the payoff constituting the ability enact or implement the policy the entrepreneur has been striving for.

In the case of the Aviation and Transportation Security Act, the budgetary largesse that was part of the post-crisis politics unlocked funds that were not available prior to the crisis. Conversely, the 2014 fire at the municipal level in Sweden created conditions of necessity for the (reactive) policy entrepreneur to find a satisfactory solution. In MSF terms, both couplings are doctrinal (policy solution in search of a problem) rather than consequential (a problem in search of a solution), which is proposed to be the norm when the window of opportunity opens in the problem stream (e.g., a crisis event) as opposed to the politics stream (e.g., elections) (Zahariadis, 2003). Policy changes tend to be formal, often involving bureaucratic reorganization, though in the case of Sri Lanka, the policy change promoted by the policy entrepreneur was informal. Even when the post-crisis policy changes are formal, policy entrepreneurial action has its limits as the establishment of the Crisis Secretariat in Sweden illustrates. Lack of political support will diminish the results of policy entrepreneurial action, even in the implementation stage.

4 Policy Entrepreneurs and Policy Outcomes in Creeping Crises

4.1 Introduction

This section chronicles three creeping crises: the Greek sovereign debt crisis 2009–2015, the COVID-19 pandemic in the US and the 2022 Russian invasion of Ukraine. By definition, the impact of such crises is predicated on structural idiosyncrasies and endogenous factors but also existing pathologies, such as not well functioning intergovernmental relations caused by a maligned federal administration (US), a low-performing public sector (Greece), or a bellicose neighbor (Ukraine). The thick description of the context of the crises provides a foundation for understanding why the crises unfolded the way it did but also to highlight the opportunity structures of actual (and in the Ukrainian case) potential policy entrepreneurs.

We follow the same template of presentation as we did in the previous section. We first provide an empirical description of the case. Then we ask and provide answers to two questions in separate parts. How do crisis challenges affect policy entrepreneurial strategies, and how do policy entrepreneurs shape policy outcomes?

4.2 The Greek Sovereign Debt Crisis, 2009–2015

When the incoming Socialist Prime Minister of Greece, George Papandreou, announced a revision to the 2009 government budget, he assumed it would be politics as usual. He followed the time-honored tradition of blaming the previous government for all the ills that befell the country but promised relief. He had a plan that would fix it all and still give the 2–5 percent wage increases that he promised to countless civil servants. The hope was to avoid blame (Hood, 2011) for the politically costly decisions that were sure to follow (Zahariadis, 2010, 2013). The problem was that his announcement of falsified budget data, the infamous "Greek statistics," came amidst the "great recession" and a global financial crisis. Uncertainty over Greek figures (expressed repeatedly by incoming governments and the Commission since 2005) resulted in a downgrade of Greece's sovereign debt by Fitch, Standard & Poor's, and Moody's driving up borrowing costs.

Desperate efforts by the Greeks to pacify world markets over the government's borrowing capacity failed miserably. The crisis was also exacerbated by the lack of solidarity among European Union (EU) members who could not agree whether it was a national or supranational (EU) problem (Featherstone, 2011). Some member states led by Germany argued against help, mainly because of domestic opposition. Others, led by the Commission, saw the danger of a Greek bankruptcy, and called for an EU-level response. In the end, the course of events forced everyone's hand.

On April 23, 2010, Eurostat increased its estimate of Greece's budget deficit to 13.6 per cent, triggering a rise of Greece's two-year bonds to 10 per cent. Unable to borrow on such terms, Greece informed its partners that it was activating the rescue package, invoking Article 122(2), which allows aid in case of emergency. The package (known as the Memorandum of Understanding, MoU) involved the gigantic amount of EUR110b over three years – EUR80b in bilateral loans and EUR30b by the IMF – monitored and disbursed quarterly on the basis of progress on specific indicators assessed by the IMF, the ECB, and the European Commission (the so-called troika). The point was to temporarily help Greece generate primary surplus to meet obligations to external creditors at a reasonable interest rate. In return, Greece agreed to a series of painful measures designed to reduce its public sector, cut salaries and pensions, and increase tax revenues through VAT tax hikes on all goods and services in addition to more taxes on tobacco, gas and alcohol, and better collection processes. Members of the cabinet later admitted that they had neither read and nor assessed the rescue package in its entirety before voting on it (Zahariadis, 2013, p. 107). Greek voters were stunned, confused, and angry.

Two years later, the crisis was repeated as Greece asked for another bailout loan. The painful measures contained in the first MoU did not yield the expected benefits. Creditors refused. Prime Minister Papandreou called for a referendum to ask Greek voters whether they agreed to the bailout's terms. The EU allies were incensed because they knew what the outcome would be. In a rare show of power, they "forced" the Prime Minister to resign, triggering a national crisis. A temporary technocratic government was installed to negotiate a new package, leaving implementation to the winner of national elections in 2012. The conservative-socialist coalition that won could not implement the terms effectively triggering yet another national and EU crisis because a new rescue plan was needed.

In January 2015, the Radical Left (SYRIZA) wins national elections and forms a coalition government with the far right on the platform of rescinding austerity and changing "Europe." The ensuing negotiations failed miserably causing more consternation and a severe economic crisis in Greece. At the end, a third three-year bailout package of up to EUR86b was negotiated with terms, such as running a budget surplus, that the country needs to abide by until 2060.

How Do Crisis Challenges Affect Policy Entrepreneurial Strategies?

The sovereign debt crisis was a monumental event for Greece and the EU as a whole. As a result, it attracted the attention of two sets of policy entrepreneurs, some of whom were more visible than others. The first set includes national policymakers, and the second set includes international policymakers. The fact that the crisis included three rescue packages that contained a combination of bilateral, multilateral, and private loans (in the form of discounts) suggests a complex web of individuals whose strategic behavior came into sharp conflict with one another.

In the first bailout package, two domestic actors, the Prime Minister George Papandreou and his Finance Minister, Giorgos Papakonstantinou, played the pivotal role in asking for the bailout package, framing the terms in politically acceptable ways, to the extent they could, and more importantly shape its implementation. We use the term coalition-building strategies to refer to implementation and link two strategies in the way Mintrom (2019b) acknowledges: using and expanding networks and working with advocacy coalitions. On the creditor side, Poul Mathias Tomsen of the IMF, and the German Chancellor, Angela Merkel, played a pivotal role in dictating the terms of the rescue. The strategies of the domestic actors worked well, to the extent that the country was financially rescued, but their framing and coalition-building (implementation) strategies were poorly executed. They were never able to "sell" the austerity package to the wider public as a rescue operation necessary for better days ahead. Instead, many people blamed them for "leading" the country into austerity. Secondly, they never "owned" the reforms they were implementing. Such blame avoidance not only enabled government officials and the public alike to evade taking the painful measures, but it also gave rise serious concerns with accountability of the political elite and the sense of communal moral responsibility (Theodossopoulos, 2013). Austerity measures simply resulted in a country at war with itself.

The crisis suited the external creditors quite nicely. The IMF representative, Mr. Tomsen, framed the rescue package as yet another usual but necessary fiscal stabilization scheme like the many that the IMF advises for developing countries. Chancellor Merkel was able to frame it as a necessary act to save the euro by rescuing the "lazy Greeks," which is an image shared by much of German public opinion at the time. The framing strategy was politically and monetarily costly but ultimately successful in that it allowed diversion from the point that by saddling the Greeks with more debt (the rescue plan consisted of loans) Germany was also saving German banks. Indeed, the majority of Greece's sovereign debt was owed to German, French, and British banks (Zahariadis, 2010).

The second package of roughly EUR109b involved mostly the same set of actors and somewhat the same strategies. On the domestic side were a Greek technocratic interim government led by former central banker Loukas Papademos, which negotiated the plan and a right-left grand coalition that implemented it led by Prime Minister Antonis Samaras. On the external side, it was the same actors, the IMF and Germany, taking the lead. However, there was one difference. Although the second rescue package involved mainly the same terms and austerity measures, it did involve a heavy discount of the country's debt to private investors by 50 per cent, for example, EU banks and other financial institutions. The creditors as well as the Greek government were able to negotiate a so-called Private Sector Involvement (PSI) settlement as a strict conditionality to the voluntary contribution of the private sector in the country's debt burden-sharing. The rescue plan eventually failed as the Greek government was unable to build coalitions and networks to implement austerity successfully although the PSI worked well for the banks because it reduced their exposure to Greek debt.

The third package involved a somewhat different set of actors and strategies. The IMF was no longer part of the rescue plan and the new Greek governing coalition of the Radical Left and Far Right sought to renegotiate the terms but ran afoul to EU institutional rules (Tsebelis, 2015). The domestic actors led by Greek Finance Minister Yanis Varoufakis and supported by Prime Minister Alexis Tsipras framed the problem as one of dignity for the Greeks and sought to completely overhaul the austerity measures demanded by the creditors (Zahariadis, 2016). The creditors led by German Finance Minister *Wolfgang Schäuble and Jean Claude Juncker, then President of the European Commission, framed it as a matter of survival for the eurozone. Eventually, the creditors succeeded in dictating the terms and convincing the Greeks to build coalitions to implement the package.*

How Do Policy Entrepreneurs Shape Policy Outcomes?

Policy entrepreneurs played a major role in shaping policy outcomes in the sovereign debt crisis. Because they were highly salient issues, both the debt crisis and rescue plans were agreed upon by major policymakers, who ended up being the policy entrepreneurs. The crisis also brought to the fore another important aspect of crisis management: the differentiation between domestic and international entrepreneurs. Domestic entrepreneurs play the most visible role but have the least power to shape outcomes. The reason is because the terms of the rescue plans were dictated by external forces. The country was practically bankrupt and needed help. Initially, solidarity was not forthcoming, relying instead on Article 125 of the Treaty on the Functioning of the European Union that maintained member states in the Eurozone did not have to rescue other members in trouble. But eventually, it became obvious that financial interdependence because of the euro necessitated a bailout of Greece and later others, such as Ireland, Portugal, and Cyprus.

The ability of domestic actors to shape the terms may have been limited but their ability to frame the rescue's policy image and build coalitions during implementation was pivotal. In other words, the most significant effects were not in agenda setting or decision-making but in implementation, at least initially. In the first two bailout packages, policymakers tried to avoid the political cost associated with painful austerity. The rescue packages were framed as imposed by outsiders, which of course generated anger and political pushback. The third package was different in that it was the Greek government's actions that shaped the policy outcome, that is, the third bailout. Interestingly, it was the far left-right coalition that was most successful in implementing the austerity measures envisaged in the bailout package. Taking a page from US President Nixon's playbook, the same politicians, who took to the streets against the sale of residences, privatization of state assets, and high taxes amidst steep austerity only three years before, successfully implemented the most far-reaching austerity measures amidst the most severe social and economic crisis in Greek memory that involved record-high unemployment and capital controls. Overall, coalition building, reputational benefits (they had previously argued fiercely against austerity), and some coercion helped turned the tide and shape the outcome.

4.3 The COVID-19 Pandemic in the US, 2020–2022

Public health in the United States is a shared responsibility between the federal, state, and local governments (DeLeo, 2010; Gostin et al., 2020). This means that public health policy in the United States is largely fragmented and is highly variable from state to state and even at the local level (Kettl, 2020; Stivers, 2022). Public health is a low salience issue for most people at most times because most of the time, the public health system works to prevent major disease outbreaks. The federal government's role is to support state and local efforts to promote public health, particularly in situations where threats to public health are national in scope. The COVID pandemic clearly fit this standard. In this way, the federal government's role is similar to its role in response to natural disasters, where the federal government supports state and local actions to mitigate to and respond to disasters, particularly when these events outstrip state and local capabilities (Kapucu and Hu, 2022; Parker and Stern, 2022).

When the first news of a novel virus originating in China became widely known, an existing public health system was mobilized at the international, national, and subnational level, which all had plans in place to handle such an event. Had the COVID pandemic been managed roughly according to the plans laid out for a pandemic, the CDC would have effectively tracked the spread of the disease across the world and into the United States, it would have developed effective tests and treatment protocols, and the federal government would have coordinated efforts to purchase and distribute supplies and equipment to hard-hit areas based on needs (Kapucu and Hu, 2022). These plans developed from experiences such as the SARS outbreak in 2002-2004 and when the H5N1 (avian) influenza became an issue of concern in the early 2002s (DeLeo, 2010, 2016).

During the transition between the Obama and Trump administrations, the Obama administration developed a "playbook" for pandemic response that it shared with the incoming Trump administration officials. The new administration largely ignored this plan (Parker and Stern, 2022), which meant that the administration largely treated the pandemic with ad hoc efforts that did little to support local response. Indeed, the mixed messages and bungled response meant that the federal government was remarkably unprepared to help, even after having learned some important lessons about disease and pandemic preparedness with SARS and MERS in the early 2000s. Instead of drawing on this experience, the Trump administration falsely claimed that the pandemic was so unprecedented that it could not have been effectively anticipated (Parker and Stern, 2022). The COVID pandemic was indeed widespread, but not so much so that the plans made in the Bush and Obama administrations would have been useless.

COVID clearly outstripped local public health efforts to track the spread of the COVID virus and to "flatten the curve," the term used to describe the pressing need to reduce the number of cases before they overwhelmed hospitals and clinics. Along these lines, the federal government was ineffective in helping states secure needed supplies and equipment, such as testing materials and ventilators for patients on intensive care. This meant that, to an extent greater than had been contemplated in pre-pandemic planning, the federal government was particularly poorly prepared to support state and local government.

To a considerable extent, this meant that state and local governments were either left to their own devices (Parker and Stern, 2022), competing with the federal government and with each other to get needed resources (Birkland et al., 2021; Kettl, 2020) or had considerable latitude for experimentation and improvisation (Congleton, 2023), depending on one's perspective. Adding to this complexity is the high degree of political polarization in the United States and its challenges to federalism (Birkland et al., 2021; Konisky and Nolette, 2021).

However, it is important not to overstate the extent to which partisanship and polarization influenced early responses to the pandemic. State governors were compelled to take action in the pandemic because the federal government under Donald Trump did not assert the sort of effective leadership that would be expected in a pandemic. Furthermore, governors were foremost actors in their states because legislatures were not in session or the legislative process was too slow, and governors had considerable power to issue executive orders (Weissert et al., 2021). For example, between March 19 (California) and April 7, 2020 (South Carolina), 43 states issued some form of form of stay-at-home order that would include, among other things, school closings, closings of non-essential businesses, and restrictions on public gatherings. Beyond stay-at-home orders, some states issued guidance or mask mandates on mask wearing, and later in the pandemic, states developed policies to promote vaccination. But states also rescinded their pandemic measures at different rates. All in all, residents of the states rated their governor higher on trustworthiness compared with President Trump (Weissert et al., 2021).

The degree to which states adopted similar policies is remarkable. While the substance of policies was more similar than some had assumed, governors made strategic choices on issues like stay-at-home orders or the reopening of businesses to signal to key constituencies the governor's policy stances. In this way, governors were largely acting politically and strategically. For example, Governors Jay Inslee of Washington State and Gavin Newsom were early and vocal adopters of measures to mitigate the pandemic based on their claims that their decisions were grounded in science. But at the same time, Florida, led by Governor Ron DeSantis, adopted a number of similar measures as other states to slow the spread of the pandemic, although the governor was much less vocal in his promotion of these policies.

Republican governors, and their supporters, by and large, chose to deemphasize the pandemic and emphasized instead the economic costs of business shutdowns, with the result that, later in the pandemic, states led by Republican governors had higher case rates and lower testing rates than did states with Democratic governors (Neelon et al., 2021). Governors of states where Trump was more popular, such as Kim Reynolds of Iowa or Ron DeSantis of Florida, were particularly unwilling to sound any greater alarm about the pandemic than was Trump.

However, while much has been made of the role of partisanship and polarization in the United States in the disparate responses of the states, once one controls for other factors, such as urban or rural residents or the age of the population, these differences fall away. And there were Republican Governors, such as Michael DeWine of Ohio, Larry Hogan of Maryland, and Charlie Baker of Massachusetts, who were also highly public proponents of science-based policies, such as social distancing and vaccination, to respond to the challenge of the pandemic (Gasulla et al., 2023).

An example of strategic innovation on the part of governors was the formation of interstate alliances that fell short of formal "interstate compacts" of the sort permitted under the Constitution. For example, Washington, Oregon, and California formed a collaborative alliance, as did "a coalition of seven mostly Northeastern states; and a Midwestern alliance" (Huq, 2020) led by the governors of Illinois, Michigan, Ohio, Wisconsin, Minnesota, Indiana and Kentucky (NBC News Chicago, 2020) These alliances shared ideas about how to reopen their states and how they could ensure sufficient health care capacity to deal with a resurgence.

In another example of strategic decision-making, Governor Ron DeSantis of Florida, clearly harboring presidential ambitions, was particularly aggressive about "protecting" the "freedoms" of Floridians by promoting legislation, that, among other things, sought to "permanently [prohibit] COVID-19 vaccine passports in Florida," or "permanently [prohibit] 'COVID-19 masking requirements at businesses.'" and banning hiring or firing decisions based on vaccination status. These prohibitions were largely symbolic, given that there was little chance of these policies becoming law in Florida (Office of Governor Ron DeSantis, 2023). Many of Governor DeSantis's claims were false and misleading, such as his and his Surgeon General's claims that mRNA vaccines were ineffective (Nehamas and LaFraniere, 2023) or even dangerous (Sarkissian, 2023). But Governors like Desantis have learned that these sorts of appeals are attractive to a particular segment of the electorate, particularly for leaders who have ambitions for higher office.

This was also true of three governors with a reputation for stringent policy responses to the pandemic. In California, Washington, and New York, governors adopted strict stay-at-home orders, encouraged school closings, and promoted vaccination. Gov. Gavin Newsom of California relied on harnessing public-private partnerships, working to support community-based organizations in California (Office of Governor Gavin Newsom, 2021). He also controversially tasked Blue Shield, a health insurance company, with the distribution of COVID vaccines, relying more heavily on the private sector than did other states because of known shortcomings in California's public health systems (Colliver, 2021). Indeed, in retrospective of his performance in the pandemic, Gov. Newsom expressed some doubts about the stringency of his state's response in the face of criticisms from other national figures, such as Gov.

DeSantis (Cadelago, 2023). Governor Jay Inslee of Washington was among the earliest proponents for strict COVID mitigation strategies, and Washington state mandated vaccines for state employees. Washington's early action was driven the emergence of the nation's first COVID case in suburban Seattle. There was little support in his state for restricting the emergency powers of the governor (Bernstein, 2023), in contrast with significant opposition in states like Michigan, where the state Supreme Court ruled unanimously that the governor's continued emergency declarations ran afoul of state emergency management law (Van Beek, 2020).

New York Governor Andrew Cuomo also played a very public role in promoting stringent anti-COVID measures. But being such a public proponent of policies comes with considerable risks if one's performance is found to fall short of their rhetoric. In New York, evidence emerged that Governor Cuomo, who pressed nursing homes to accept COVID patients when hospitals were full, pressed officials to hide the rates of illness and deaths in nursing homes (Cohrs, 2021). In covering up the nursing home data, Gov. Cuomo squandered a great deal of political capital and goodwill. He was ultimately forced to resign as governor over other sexual harassment issues, but the coverup of the data combined with his behavior made his position untenable (Ferré-Sadurní and Goodman, 2021).

How Do Crisis Challenges Affect Policy Entrepreneurial Strategies?

The literature on policy entrepreneurs notes that elected officials can be policy entrepreneurs. What distinguishes the elected officials highlighted in this section is their acting operationally – managing a public health response – but also acting strategically and politically. The positions they took were intended to appeal to constituencies and to position themselves for reelection, for candidacy for higher office, or for the development of political capital that could be useful in other policy debates. By contrast, appointed officials and civil servants, depending on their role, were more concerned with operational aspects of the public health system, and tended to frame their goals in terms of control of the effects of the pandemic. At the federal level, the most prominent civil servant policy entrepreneur was Dr. Anthony Fauci, director of the National Institute of Allergy and Infectious Diseases in the National Institutes of Health. Dr. Fauci was an early and very public figure in providing advice to the administration– and providing a counterweight to the Trump Administration's more questionable claims – with an eye toward reducing the rate of infections, and therefore reducing demand on hospitals, until a vaccine became effective. He then became a very effective public proponent of vaccination (Taylor et al., 2023).

Dr. Fauci was working at two different levels during the pandemic: within government, seeking to provide useful information to decision makers, and outside of government, serving as symbol of the medical profession and using his highly visible position to encourage public behaviors that would slow the spread of the virus. Indeed, Taylor et al. (2023) found that Dr. Fauci was notably influential in the behavior of political conservatives as he became a national symbol of the public health system as it was supposed to work, in contrast with the fumbling response by the Centers for Disease Control and, of course, the confused, at best, messaging coming from President Trump and his closest advisors (Dawsey and Abutaleb, 2020). Of course, this did not mean that Dr. Fauci was completely free to act, although his status as a senior federal civil servant – not as a political appointee – gave him a degree of protection from retaliation that other officials did not enjoy (Villegas, 2020). But it did mean that, as the pandemic continued through 2020 and before the presidential election, his role as an advocate *within* the White House – where he briefed officials almost daily in the early phase of the pandemic – became less prominent as the administration sought to prioritize reopening the economy. But he was an effective communicator among the public; he invested his time and put at stake his reputation and experience to, as he said, "stand up for the data and evidence and facts and science" (Park, 2022).

At the state and local level, highly placed public health officials also were policy entrepreneurs, who invested their time and experience to share their advice for the public. An example is Dr. Mandy Cohen, the Secretary of the North Carolina Department of Health and Human Services from 2017 to 2022. As an appointed state official, she worked closely with Governor Roy Cooper and, like Fauci, was an effective communicator and policy advisor that worked to "flatten the curve" of COVID infections. This notion of "flattening the curve" was a priority shared by most public health officials at the state and local level, who confronted the very real possibility that hospitals could be overwhelmed. Dr. Cohen became the daily face of the pandemic for North Carolinians, supported by Gov. Cooper. As a news story noted, Dr. Cohen had "been preparing for this moment for the past two decades, since a summer in Washington, D.C., ignited her interest in the intersection of health care, policy and medicine" (Carter, 2020). In this way, Dr. Cohen was the sort of policy analyst and entrepreneur that Radin (2013) wrote about in her description of the new type of policy analyst, one that can combine policymaking savvy with technical knowledge to become an effective advocate.

Entrepreneurial strategies in American policymaking are shaped and challenged by the inherent fragmentation of American politics coupled with growing partisan polarization. Many treatments of American federalism treat the polycentric organization of governments as a positive feature of American governance – the so-called "laboratories of democracy" – but it also means that policy entrepreneurs working at the federal level will not uniformly influence public health nationally, as reflected by the substantial differences in outcomes at the state level (Neelon et al., 2021). This means that there were numerous venues available for policy entrepreneurs at the federal and state levels to pursue both political and policy goals; those political goals were sometimes antithetical to the promotion of good pandemic management. In any event, governors and others working as policy entrepreneurs adopted scaling up change processes within a state and between states. For example, the effort to develop multi-state alliances to coordinate pandemic response was a way for governors and their health officials to coordinate activity. This entrepreneurial activity was particularly important in light of concerns raised by elected and appointed officials that the Trump administration was not taking the pandemic seriously, or that the administration wrongly believed the pandemic would quickly be controlled. National policy entrepreneurs such as Anthony Fauci also had to contend with the remarkable degree of variability in state policies. Even though all but six states did issue some form of stay-at-home order in the last few weeks of March and the first week of April 2000, the stringency of the overall measures taken by the states and the variability in the number of policy tools they used meant that there were remarkable state-by-state differences in outcomes (Birkland et al., 2021; Taylor et al., 2022). We can therefore think of scaling up as being hierarchical in an organization, but we can also think of scaling up in terms of the scope of influence that the policy entrepreneur wants to exercise; governors both scaled up to the federal level, pressing for federal support for states, as well as outward to other states to seek support for their efforts.

Governors and public health officials also demonstrated how they were "using and expanding networks." to respond to the crisis. Dr. Fauci was a leading figure in a vast network of public health officials at the national and state levels, while governors' attempts to harness connections through ad-hoc regional alliances, as well as established institutions such as the National Governors' Association, were evidence of entrepreneurial actions. Indeed, given the nature of federalism and public health in the United States, it would be difficult for a policy entrepreneur to be effective outside these existing networks. Governors, in particular, were already part of important networks at the state and national level through political parties, relations with the congressional delegation, and their extensive personal networks. Along these lines, Mintrom also notes that successful policy entrepreneurs work through existing advocacy coalitions. For example, Drs. Fauci and Cohen worked within a broader public health advocacy coalition that was activated during the pandemic to press for effective measures to contain the COVID pandemic. Networking, scaling up change processes, and working with advocacy coalitions were all related to each other and were clearly important to policy entrepreneurs.

Another important strategy is problem framing. Leading governors, as well as Drs. Fauci and Cohen framed the COVID problem as a severe threat to public health to justify taking aggressive steps to control the pandemic. Other governors, such as Ron DeSantis of Florida, and Kim Reynolds of Iowa, began to downplay the severity of the pandemic, framing the problems caused by the pandemic in terms of damage to the economy or as disruptive to other goals, such as education, rather than as ongoing threats to public health. Policy entrepreneurs thus engaged in framing battles to shape the stringency and duration of COVID control policies.

These are all common strategies common to policy entrepreneurs' success. The COVID crisis did not change these strategies but made the pace of activity much quicker and the stakes involved much higher as participants in policy-making learned and changed their positions in real time, with little time for deliberation. For example, early in the pandemic, Dr. Fauci downplayed to some extent the likelihood of it becoming severe, and early in the pandemic seemed to downplay the utility of face masks, positions that came back to haunt him later as elected officials challenged his credibility. But Dr. Fauci demonstrates that policy entrepreneurs must risk their credibility and their reputations at times to achieve their goals. These risks are amplified during crises, when the public seeks reassurance and officials seek quick and, hopefully, easy answers to difficult problems.

How Do Policy Entrepreneurs Shape Policy Outcomes?

Policy entrepreneurs in the United States shaped policy outcomes by often taking very different positions, with Republican governors, for the most part, being less active in policymaking than were Democratic governors, with notable exceptions. What resulted was a great deal of experimentation, both in terms of the actual policies adopted to address the pandemic and, from a political perspective, the kinds of arguments that were harnessed by elected officials and senior bureaucrats to attempt to control the pandemic or, in some states, to deemphasize the pandemic and focus on other goals, like the preservation of the economy. This slow-burning crisis meant that policy entrepreneurs needed to be nimble and to change their approaches and their recommendations as new information came to light about the pandemic and the prospects for containing and weathering it.

4.4 The Russian Invasion of Ukraine, 2022

After several weeks of intense accusations by the world community of an impending invasion of Ukraine and strong Russian denials, the inevitable happened on February 24, 2022. Russian troops overran Ukrainian positions along the Russo- and Belarusian-Ukrainian borders, resulting in an invasion that was the biggest attack on a European country since World War II. The crisis was years in the making, stemming from differences that some take back to the time of the czars and even before then.

Many Russian politicians consider Ukraine to be part of Russia's historical space (see Putin's article in Domanska (2021) where he claims Ukraine to be an inseparable part of the "triune Russian nation"). In fact, they track commonalities to the establishment of the Kyivan Rus empire in the tenth century AD and the many centuries of Russification that ensued under the Czars. However, politically speaking, the real issues begin with the Russian Revolution in 1917, in which the nationalist government in Kyiv sided against the Bolsheviks during the civil war. The Bolsheviks established control in 1919 and declared Ukraine a Soviet Republic, with Ukrainian as the official language. Following the horrible famine of the 1930s, in which an estimated 4-5 million Ukrainians perished, Nazi occupation revealed political resentment and ethnic fissures lying dormant under the communist facade. Some Ukrainians joined the resistance, some fought for independence against the Nazis and Soviets, and still others collaborated with the Nazis. When Ukraine became an independent state in 1991, following the dissolution of the Soviet Union, issues arose about the fate of the Crimea peninsula – an area transferred to Ukraine by Soviet General Secretary Nikita Khrushchev in 1953 – and left-over nuclear weapons in the newly formed state. Russian involvement in Ukrainian politics became overt in 2005, during the Orange Revolution, and again in 2014 with the annexation of Crimea. Russian concern in the region was heightened again when discussions took place with the European Union (EU) about the possibility of Ukraine joining the EU-27 in 2021. Following mobilization of Russian troops along the Russo-Ukrainian borders and within neighboring Belarus, Russian President Vladimir Putin finally gave the green light to invade Ukraine in February 2022. The war and ensuing crisis have continued unabated to the present day with devastating consequences worldwide.

How Do Crisis Challenges Affect Policy Entrepreneurial Strategies?

Most of the literature on crises in foreign policy asserts that crisis decision-making involves mainly high-level politicians and their close advisors (e.g., Garrison, 2017; Allison, 1971). Foreign policy is generally not permeated by societal actors, making it an elite and rather closed off exercise that differs significantly from domestic policy. This case is similar in this regard. Two types of policy entrepreneurs are involved: *participants* to the crisis, such as Russian President Vladimir Putin and Ukrainian President Volodymyr Zelensky, and (not just disinterested) *outside observers*, such as US President Joe Biden, German Chancellor Olaf Scholz, Turkish President Recep Tayyip Erdoğan, and Chinese President Xi Jinping. While the military is unmistakably involved, the fate of several generals and "strong men" in Russia, such as Yevgeny Prigozhin, casts doubt on their lasting impact. And the US and British intelligence communities played a key role in providing information about the impending Russian invasion and in helping to shape NATO's response (Eckel, 2023). Much like the Greek sovereign debt crisis above, the entrepreneurial strategies involved framing the crisis in advantageous terms and coalition-building.

Politicians in the two warring states worked their hardest to frame the war in advantageous terms both domestically and abroad. While both appear to have had considerable success in the domestic front, only President Zelensky has been able to claim success internationally. The crucial concern is crafting a narrative about the essence of the crisis. President Putin has called the war a "special (limited) military operation" conducted by "peacekeepers" against the "Nazis" running Ukraine. Russia, according to its permanent representative to the UN, was acting in self-defense (Schmitt, 2022). In contrast, President Zelensky defined it as an invasion against which Ukrainians will defend themselves. In a televised broadcast to Russians hours before the invasion, he said: "Your leaders approved them [thousands of Russian soldiers] to make a step forward, to the territory of another country. And this step can be the beginning of a big war on the European continent" (Al-Jazeera, 2022). While both aimed at swaying public opinion on the other side, they have naturally been far more successful domestically (Weir, 2022). This is because at a time of extreme crisis, each leader controls the narrative in his country.

Crisis challenges, however, have forced participants to seek outside help. Participants need to convince citizens in non-direct participant countries that they are right to put pressure on these countries' leadership to act (or not) in a politically advantageous way. President Zelensky has been far more successful in the West in doing so. In contrast to the Russian takeover of Crimea and troubles in the Donbas region in 2014, the Ukrainian leadership in 2022 has framed the war in a way that has not only brought significant military assistance for Ukraine, but also raised condemnation and economic punishment of Russia. It has acted decisively and speedily and has used many public relations firms and other lobby groups in the United States and Europe – such as Yorktown Solutions, KARV

Communications, Ogilvy, Hills & Knowlton Strategies – to successfully influence policy (Fuchs, 2022; Oprysko, 2022). President Biden went so far in his support of Ukraine to call the war a "battle between democracy and autocracy" (Euronews, 2022). For his part, President Putin has been able to elicit recalcitrant statements of support from President Jinping, but mainly replace diminishing Western markets for Russian oil and gas with the Chinese market. To add to the complexity of the situation, Turkish President Erdoğan has used similar the strategy of framing the Ukraine crisis to achieve completely unrelated domestic, Turkish aims. For example, he has stalled coalition-building within the NATO alliance to get concessions from Sweden about its vocal Kurdish minority. Fearing for their security against a possible Russian invasion, governments in Sweden and Finland sought to build defense coalitions by joining NATO. However, despite universal condemnation, President Erdoğan used the Swedish application as leverage to gain concessions against Kurdish dissidents in Sweden. In essence, crisis challenges have affected participant and observer aims although the strategies used by each type remain more-or-less the same.

How Do Policy Entrepreneurs Shape Policy Outcomes?

It is too early to talk about policy outcomes because the crisis is not over. But some conclusions may be drawn as to the aims and strategies of policy entrepreneurs. First, because of the high-level status of the entrepreneurs and the substance of foreign policy, the role of entrepreneurs has been catalytic in shaping strategic responses to the crisis. In this way, we confirm the literature's findings that foreign policy is often the product of a small group of decision-makers (Garrison, 2017). Second, we uncovered two strategies, framing and coalition-building, that are common in other crises. This fact provides further support to the argument that entrepreneurs play a crucial role in framing foreign crises and shaping responses (Blavoukos and Bourantonis, 2012).

4.5 Conclusions: Creeping Crises and Public Policy Change

As we had anticipated, the long horizon of the creeping crisis resembles normal policymaking and for this reason, no significant differences exist between the two policymaking contexts. However, we argue that differences are not a matter of strategies, but a matter of emergence. The COVID-19 pandemic (ahead of a national election) mobilized state governors and spurred policy entrepreneurial action, both at the strategic and operative levels. Conversely, international entrepreneurs emerged in the Greek case, who perhaps would not have a reason to get involved had it not been for the crisis occurring. In the Ukrainian case, we offer a possible future scenario of entrepreneurial action in the foreign policy sector.

5 The Politics of Crisis Policy Entrepreneurship and a Research Agenda

5.1 Policy Entrepreneurs, Crises, and Policy Change

In this Element, we have focused on the interactions between policy entrepreneurs and crises so that we may better understand how policy entrepreneurs bring about public policy change in a crisis context. Policy entrepreneurs have been neglected in the crisis management literature, whereas crises are generally in the background, and lack nuance in the public policy scholarship. Both of these points create a knowledge gap that this Element has sought to fill. Based on the analysis of the case studies and scaffolded by the results of the literature review in Section 1, in the section that follows, we first present a framework that adds granularity to the understanding of entrepreneurial engagement in crisis events. We continue by inserting the concept of crisis into theories of the policy process. We add specificity by differentiating between fast-burning and creeping crises in the policy process. This allows us to consider specific crisis attributes when incorporating the context of crisis policymaking in theories of the policy process. We continue with avenues for future research, including methodological issues, the legitimacy of policy entrepreneurs, and the concomitant question of politicization. Finally, we discuss some potential implications for professionals in crisis management and related fields.

5.1.1 Crisis Policymaking and Policy Entrepreneurs – An Analytical Framework

Much like in normal policymaking, policy entrepreneurs have the potential to emerge during any crisis event. There are plenty of instances, of course, when no entrepreneur is present. In such instances, we would expect the status quo to prevail with no significant changes in public policy. In this section – as in the previous ones – we continue using the analytical distinction of *fast-burning* and *creeping crises*. We also differentiate between two kinds of entrepreneurs as outlined in Section 2: *proactive policy entrepreneurs*, who fit the traditional notion of the opportunity-seeking policy entrepreneur intrinsically driven by focused intentionality, and *reactive policy entrepreneurs*, who are driven by extrinsic pressures. The result is a two by two analytical framework as visualized in Figure 3. It makes knowledge claims about policymaking based on the two temporally defined crisis types and the two types of policy entrepreneurs described in Section 2.

When reactive policy entrepreneurs emerge in a fast-burning crisis event (top left quadrant of Figure 3), it is because this event has created conditions of necessity that act as extrinsic pressures exerted on the entrepreneur, creating the

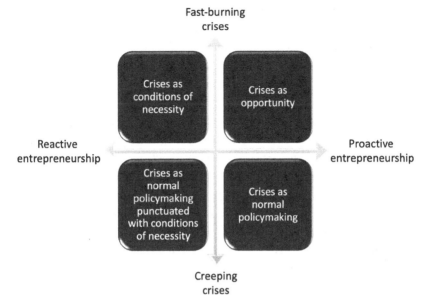

Figure 3 Crisis policymaking and policy entrepreneurs – an analytical framework

imperative for a satisficing solution within a truncated time period. Political actors may feel they have no choice but to act entrepreneurially (and this feeling of having no choice constitutes necessity) because the perceived impact of the crisis and attendant high levels of uncertainty make action – and through this action providing some solution – imperative. Much like in the market environment, this kind of entrepreneurship is less likely to result in significant change because it is the outcome of a forced choice. We expect the strategy of using and expanding networks to be prominent in the search for a satisficing solution. As shown in the case study of the forest fire in Sweden, the policy entrepreneur tapped his networks for feedback in his search for a solution to a problem he had not considered relevant before – namely, a forest fire of an unprecedented scale.

Conversely, the emergence of a proactive policy entrepreneur in a fast-burning crisis (top right quadrant of Figure 3) is perhaps the textbook case of a focusing event triggering a window of opportunity in MSF terms. These entrepreneurs have a policy solution in mind long before a crisis occurs. They are intrinsically motivated to promote their preferred policy solution and, like their market counterparts, seek and are alert to opportunities. They educate different audiences with material in traditional and social media and are instrumental in softening institutional rigidities. Entrepreneurs are ready to act when an opportunity, such as a fast-burning crisis, presents itself. Two quite different examples from the case studies illustrate this. John Ashcroft and his supporters advocated for the Patriot Act in response to the 9/11 attacks, legislation that its critics claim is an affront to civil liberties. This solution, long advocated by the Bush administration, was presented as one furthering the interest of national security – an opportunity afforded to the policy entrepreneur by the event. Similarly, the Indian Ocean tsunami presented an opportunity to Ranjith Dissanayake, the policy entrepreneur, and civil engineer in Sri Lanka, to mobilize resources for change in building practices. We expect that the most prominent entrepreneurial strategy is problem framing. All entrepreneurs must be adept at problem framing and, in these conditions, perhaps more so when policymakers must be convinced during the acute phase of the crisis during the brief period when the institutional rigidities are less resistant. As with market entrepreneurship driven by opportunity seeking, we expect policy innovation as a result.

Creeping crises are characterized by high levels of ambiguity and a relative lack of urgency. Indeed, Magnus Ekengren, in a 2023 paper, asks why governments seem to be surprised when their countries are hit by the consequences of creeping crises, including the effects of climate change or a pandemic. Despite the abundance of scientific knowledge, the urgency to act is stymied. We argue that during such crises, there exist punctuation points that focus urgency toward action. These instances may constitute conditions of necessity for reactive policy entrepreneurs (bottom left quadrant of Figure 3). Conditions of necessity may translate in practice into top-down political pressure imposed on public servants or elected officials who are called upon to ameliorate the consequences of the creeping crisis. Potential reactive entrepreneurs can be found among the governors and state health officials in the COVID-19 case study in the US outlined in Section 4. The timeframe of a creeping crisis has a longer horizon than that of a fast-burning crisis, and we hypothesize that an important policy entrepreneurial strategy under these conditions is scaling up policy change. Like in the market environment, we expect incremental change as a result of successful policy entrepreneurial action.

Finally, the emergence of proactive policy entrepreneurs in creeping crises constitutes the conditions most similar to normal policymaking (bottom right quadrant of Figure 3). Most challenges of our time, from the climate crisis to deep economic crises and armed conflicts, have been wicked problems spanning over many policy areas, ignored and left to simmer until they erupt. Crisis governance becomes everyday governance, necessitating normal policymaking. This was certainly true during the prolonged economic crisis and period of austerity in Greece, where a salient policy entrepreneurial strategy highlighted coalition building.

5.1.2 Crises in Theories of the Policy Process

Given the discussion above, we argue for the articulated theoretical insertion of a nuanced concept of crisis in theories of the policy process. Given the scope and space limitations of this Element, we focus on the theories that already include policy entrepreneurs and crises in some form, and we propose further avenues for more specificity[2].

The Multiple Streams Framework

The MSF seeks to answer the question of how policymakers select policy problems to attend to, thus elevating them to the top of the political agenda, and what policy solutions to adopt and implement (Kingdon, 2011; Zahariadis et al., 2023). In *Agendas, Alternatives, and Public Policies,* originally published in 1984, Kingdon (2011) argued that policy issues ascend to the political agenda as the result of developments in three separate process streams: the problem stream, the policy stream, and the politics stream. Most of the time, the streams operate largely independently of each other, but they converge periodically. During such periods of convergence, decision opportunities appear. Policy entrepreneurs often join these three independent streams by identifying and taking advantage of (or creating) windows of opportunity, which are often preceded by a focusing event (Herweg et al., 2023; Zahariadis, 2007). There is no *a priori* or "natural" connection between problems and solutions (Herweg et al., 2023), much the same way in which there is no objective definition of a threat (Boin et al., 2017). For this reason, a policy entrepreneur must be present to couple the streams.

Arguably, MSF includes the most developed treatment of crises in the "focusing event" concept. Inserting a nuanced understanding of crises in the framework would add more analytical leverage to the problem stream, the window of opportunity, and entrepreneurial action. For example, identifying a reactive policy entrepreneur in action and a creeping crisis as a focusing event might explain the lack of dynamic change even after the streams are coupled within the window of opportunity. The type of crisis also has the potential to explain the duration of the window of opportunity, which has implications for the coupling of streams, as touched upon by Dolan (2021). Additionally, a better understanding of the focusing event based on the dynamics of different crises can contribute to a better prediction of the political relevance of a condition (Herweg et al., 2023). Herweg et al. (2015) suggest that political relevance is strongly related to the electoral relevance of a condition, that is, the attention it receives from voters. Given that crisis

---

[2] Due to space limitations, we provide only a summary description of MSF, ACF, PET, and NPF. Readers who wish a thorough discussion should refer to the latest edition of the Theories of the Policy Process and its sister publication Methods of the Policy Process.

management is event-driven, understanding which events may be of salience to voters may help clarify, in turn, the events that will be important to policymakers.

Punctuated Equilibrium Theory

Punctuated equilibrium theory conceptualizes political processes as generally characterized by stasis and incrementalism punctuated with infrequent spikes of substantial change. In this interpretation of the policymaking process, the task for advocates of policy change is to bring the policy issues into the public arena (Baumgartner et al., 2023; see also van der Dool and Li, 2023) for a review of how PET plays out in an autocracy [China]). The challenge for those seeking such change is to undermine existing present policy images and create new ones that emphasize major problems and why the status quo is not sustainable. Often, this happens by shifting the decision venue, obtained by shifting jurisdictions or levels of governance. Policy images, that is, policy narratives, have the potential to provide fertile ground for reactive and proactive policy entrepreneurs, especially when these images are conflicting. Policy entrepreneurs may be instrumental in shifting the policy venue and thus introducing change.

We argue that a better understanding of crises can inform PET because it can nuance punctuations induced by a crisis event. Baumgartner et al. (2023) suggest that though some crises are extreme and hard to predict, better governance systems that can detect crises may ameliorate the impact of such punctuations. As we have seen in this Element, there is a variety of crisis typologies that can be used to inform the timing and impact of a punctuation, as well as the attendant decision venue. Particularly useful in terms of punctuation are the dynamics of the creeping crises, especially as they relate to the question Ekengren (2024) posed regarding the element of surprise that governments exhibit when, in fact, they are aware that a crisis will hit. Understanding different types of crises can inform the ways policy systems are able to predict and prepare for punctuations.

The Advocacy Coalition Framework

Although the original scope of the ACF was limited to the US policy arena, significant revisions have increased its scope of application (Nohrsdtedt et al., 2023; Nowlin, 2011; Petridou, 2014). Entrepreneurs are able to seize opportunities while creating a positive vision for the coalition to attract additional resources and use them strategically. Within the ACF, change comes from both internal and external sources. However, to have a political effect, those catalysts for change need to be appropriately interpreted, often by policy entrepreneurs, in order to attract the policymakers' attention. Policy entrepreneurs also play a role in constructing a successful vision for coalitions.

The ACF conceptualizes a set of external subsystem events that have the potential to influence the short-term constraints and resources of subsystem actors. These include changes in socioeconomic conditions, changes in public opinion, changes in the systemic governing coalition, and changes in other policy subsystems (Nohrsdtedt et al., 2023). A crisis event may cause these changes. Understanding its dynamics and the kind of crisis the event is using an existing typology can inform the external subsystem change of the potential impact on the subsystem. Indicatively, a creeping crisis such as a recession or a prolonged pandemic places a more widespread strain on the socioeconomic conditions of the population compared to a fast-burning crisis of an extreme weather event (e.g., a flood), even though the latter may be seen as part of the larger creeping crisis of climate change.

The Narrative Policy Framework

The NPF is based on the premise that policy narratives can be studied using systematic empirical approaches, applying a standardized codebook operationalizing the setting (political context), characters (such as heroes, villains, and victims), the plot, and a moral of the story (Jones et al., 2023).[3] Salient actors within NPF are the "policy marketers." Policy marketers could emerge from various positions in and around government and "spend much of their time constructing public policy problems, defining relevant policy beliefs, and ultimately reducing complex and interrelated societal problems into simple policy marketing packages" (McBeth and Shanahan, 2004). Petridou and Mintrom (2021) argue for a direct insertion of the concept of the policy entrepreneur as a central player in the NPF. It holds the potential to further enrich the theorization of the policymaking process and guide new empirical explorations. The concept of reactive policy entrepreneurship could add to these empirical explorations with a focus on resources available to entrepreneurial actors and their importance in policy narratives. Recent work by Hand et al. (2023) continues along this vein, further exploring the overlaps between the policy entrepreneur and the narrator, the strategic actor that builds a policy narrative so that a policy solution fits a policy problem for the purpose of shaping the policy agenda. Finally, we argue that understanding a crisis context as the *setting* of a narrative has the potential to integrate different kinds of contextual conditions in the NPF codebook and thus increase their analytical leverage in the framework.

5.1.3 A Research Agenda

Preparedness for, the management of, and ultimately the normalization of crises are sociopolitical processes that involve many and diverse actors. They are

---

[3] See also https://www.narrativepolicyframework.org.

integral parts of the work actors and institutions in and around government do – or should be doing – to provide societal safety. Crisis management (including preparedness and recovery) includes development and maintaining appropriate technologies, securing political support and agency mandates, managing and curating information, and cultivating broad networks of stakeholders. These actions have traditionally been ascribed to leaders, but as we have shown in this Element, they are performed by policy entrepreneurs as well, though towards a different end; initiating and implementing innovation for the purpose of bringing about change. We propose five avenues of future research: (i) understanding the dynamics of policy entrepreneurship and leadership during crises; (ii) exploring the legitimacy of policy entrepreneurs; (iii) scrutinizing the politicization of policy entrepreneurial action; (iv) examining factors that contribute to the success of policy entrepreneurs, and (v) a focus on epistemological concerns.

Crisis Leadership and Crisis Policy Entrepreneurship

Even a cursory survey of the cases in this Element will reveal that the majority of policy entrepreneurs had leadership positions. We already know from normal policymaking that significant conceptual conflation exists between leaders and policy entrepreneurs (Capano and Galanti, 2018, 2021; Petridou, 2017). The question that arises is whether, indeed, policy entrepreneurs during crises (both creeping and fast-burning) happen to hold leadership positions or whether there is something else at play. This is a fruitful avenue for future research. First, crises affect many policy sectors at once; some policy sectors (like defense of foreign policy) operate in more restrictive subsystems with few opportunities for diverse actors to be active. Second, case studies have a retrospective quality, that is, researchers work backwards. The actors who receive attention are perhaps those who told the story of crisis management from a position of formal power. This is an epistemological issue, calling for more comparative research designs and an open mind to look for entrepreneurial action in many aspects of the crisis.

Legitimacy of Policy Entrepreneurial Action

The urgency and pressure crises engender a widening of the range of acceptable policy solutions because publics are more willing to accept government action – as opposed to governments doing nothing – which in turn provides opportunities as well as political pressure to policy entrepreneurs. Carrying out these actions while at the same time minimizing their impact on democratic processes requires legitimacy of governance. Political legitimacy refers to the acceptance and justification of political authority and power by individuals or groups within a society (Galan, 2018). It explores the basis on which a government or political system is considered valid, rightful, and deserving of the compliance of its citizens. Governance legitimacy, as it relates to crisis preparedness and management, is affected by the ability of governments to adapt and learn in order to counteract the uncertainty crises engender (Christensen et al., 2016). This concept is related to the narrower concept of the legitimacy of crisis accountability (Boin et al., 2017), which "is an intensely political process" and one that "forces elected leaders to explain what went wrong, why, and what they did to limit the consequences of failure" (p.110). Policy entrepreneurs may or may not be elected officials, and they influence the capacity of governments to adapt and learn from crisis events. The question that emerges concerns the legitimacy of policy entrepreneurs in the context of crisis policymaking. Here exists a considerable gap in the literature, which tends to be very normative (though see Garsten, 2022; Lewis, 1980). Policy entrepreneurs, much like their market counterparts, are infused with positive connotations – they are energetic, and they drive innovation and dynamic change in public policy. Who, after all, dares be against innovation?

We, therefore, propose that future research on policy entrepreneurial action in crisis contexts adopt a critical perspective on the legitimacy of the entrepreneurial process as well as the legitimacy of its outcome. Case study, experimental, and comparative research may be accommodated in this endeavor. Here, we offer an example of how this future research trajectory may be inserted in the scholarship of a creeping crisis such as the COVID-19 pandemic (see Section 4) in which expert knowledge and the legitimacy of such knowledge played a salient role. Actors included in such research would involve the experts and public servants who engendered knowledge and problem frames as well as the public discourse surrounding it. A similar design could be followed in other creeping crises in which expert knowledge plays a key role.

Key factors for the legitimation of knowledge claims and problem frames include the authority and credibility of experts and potential policy entrepreneurs, as well as the perceived validity of the decision-making process informed by these knowledge claims and attendant problem frames. Evidence-based decision-making plays a particularly prominent role in ensuring the legitimacy of health policies. However, a host of cognitive and institutional biases might influence the interpretation of evidence during a pandemic, including routines, bureaucratic practices, mental models (sensemaking), confirmation bias (filtering the world through prior experience), and emotions (Rubin et al., 2021). A fruitful study along these lines would, at the first stage, identify policy entrepreneurs and, at the second stage, examine the process through which these entrepreneurs legitimize expert knowledge in the way they make meaning of the crisis.

Politicization of Policy Entrepreneurs

A related question concerns the politicization of policy entrepreneurs. The departure point of this discussion is that politicization, as Hay (2007) notes, is a contested term that has both negative and positive connotations. Here, we would like to focus on the negative aspects of politicization and recognize recent research that takes up the politicization of bureaucracies during increasing levels of populistic regimes as a possible avenue for further research connected to the legitimacy of policy entrepreneurial action (Peters and Pierre, 2022). Peters and Pierre (2022) argue that the rise of populist regimes has come with attempts to politicize the bureaucracy and has resulted in democratic backsliding, that is, undermining democratic values even in liberal democracies. They define populism as a "set of policy preferences that favor some groups in society, especially the native-born and 'average citizens' as opposed to elites" (Peters and Pierre, p. 631), whereas politicization of bureaucracy is understood to be a state in which political criteria are used to select, retain, promote, reward, and discipline public servants (Peters and Pierre, 2004).

Public service is important when it comes to crisis management because it is part of public administration – Woodrow Wilson's idea of *government in action* (1888). Politicized policy entrepreneurs who support populist regimes have the potential to further erode minority rights during the times in which they are most vulnerable, that is, during a crisis. Conversely, politicized policy entrepreneurs who refuse to implement populist policies and strive for policy innovation geared toward equity face their own theoretical and practical questions relating to the legitimate autonomy of public service during both normal and extraordinary times.

Success of Policy Entrepreneurs

A fourth question that emerges, one that has persisted within the policy entrepreneurship literature, concerns the success of policy entrepreneurial action. Both policy research and research on crises and crisis management are (to some extent) dominated by case studies. There are good reasons for this. The importance of context is hard to overestimate when it comes to the ability of knowledge claims regarding public policy and crises to travel, while the thick description of individual crisis events allows for practical and theoretical lessons (see Boin et al., 2008; Stillman, 2005). Additionally, research on policy entrepreneurs often starts backward: the researcher identifies a significant change and works backward to the policy entrepreneurial action that made it possible. To alleviate the potential selection bias of choosing successful policy entrepreneurs because their actions led to change in a crisis context, we follow Petridou and Mintrom (2021) in suggesting a more robust research design, namely a multi-variate design involving the presence or absence of policy entrepreneurs, the presence or absence of change, and the type of crisis based on the different typologies in the literature. This type of design can get complicated, but it is a way to understand the relationship between policy entrepreneurial action, when it becomes successful (policy change), and during which types of crisis.

A Focus on Method

Finally, experimental design involving simulation experiments and observational studies has shown promise in crisis management studies (see Petridou et al., 2024). Simulation policy experiments involving decision-makers might be designed to include a variety of policy solution scenarios tied to different types of crises. Such experiments may be designed to measure the correlation between policy entrepreneurial action and different types of crises. Measuring the policy entrepreneur has so far been understood in binary terms (in other words, one is an entrepreneur or not), but exciting and promising work by Arnold et al., 2023) points to ways to measure, and thus nuance, the policy entrepreneur.

5.2 Crisis Policy Entrepreneurship: Lessons for Crisis Managers

In this Element, we have attempted to shed light on the politics of crisis policy entrepreneurship and the interactions between policy entrepreneurs and crises. We conclude this book with a final question: what does this all mean in practice, if anything? In our long experience in this field, we have met creative people in and around government who work in the public sector or are part of civil society out of a public service ethos, driven by the desire to make a difference in local, national, or international crisis management efforts. Becoming an energetic actor pursuing policy innovation during crises has the potential to bring about change in tackling the grand challenges of our time, including, for example, the climate crisis. The room for action afforded to policy entrepreneurs depends on the policy sector (defense policy, e.g., is a more closed subsystem than environmental policy), level of governance, the strategic vs. operative dimension of crisis management, and, of course, type of crisis. In this final section of the Element, we revisit the policy entrepreneurial challenges in crisis contexts outlined in Section 2.

Much like leaders, policy entrepreneurs are called upon to make sense of the crisis. Policy entrepreneurs must be alert to weak signals of extraordinary events and make sense of them so that they are able to formulate suitable solutions. A haphazard understanding of a crisis may lead to an expensive and chaotic response. To some extent, this challenge is contextualized so that the policy entrepreneur must be politically astute when making sense of the crisis for their organization.

Meaning-making is another challenge that policy entrepreneurs share with leaders. Crisis managers who wish to act entrepreneurially must be able to tell a good story. Knowing one's audience contributes to effective meaning-making. A dialectic approach can ensure that the narrative of the crisis is nuanced, fitting different audiences (citizens, policymakers), and told for different purposes. Regardless, the arguments policy entrepreneurs make must be credible and persuasive.

Policy entrepreneurs must be versed in navigating the politics of governance. While creeping crises afford time for coalition building, fast-burning crises may blindside entrepreneurs who have not built coalitions. Successful policy entrepreneurs in a crisis policy context must be continuously tending to their networks and coalitions. Finally, policy entrepreneurs must be able to upscale (vertically and laterally) innovation. The one recurring lamentation in the crisis management and disaster resilience communities at the local, national, and supranational levels is that actors involved in crisis preparedness and management work in silos. Overcoming fragmentation can amplify and institutionalize policy innovation. Current crises, fast-burning and creeping alike, require the ability to harness change. Understanding policy entrepreneurial action may help us do just that.

References

Aberbach, J. D., & Christensen, T. 2001. Radical Reform in New Zealand: Crisis, Windows of Opportunity, and Rational Actors. *Public Administration.* 79(2):403–422.

Al-Jazeera. 2022. Russia-Ukraine Crisis: Zelenskyy's Address in Full. Retrieved on February 24, 2023. www.aljazeera.com/news/2022/2/24/russia-ukraine-crisis-president-zelenskky-speech-in-full.

Almond, G. A., Flanagan, S., and Mundt, S. (eds). (1973). *Crisis, Choice, and Change.* Boston: Little Brown.

Allison, G. T. 1971. *Essence of Decision.* Boston: Little Brown.

Anderson, S. E., DeLeo, R. A., & Taylor, K. 2019. Policy Entrepreneurs, Legislators, and Agenda Setting: Information and Influence. *Policy Studies Journal.* 48(3):587–611.

Angulo-Guerrero, M. J., Pérez-Moreno, S., & Abad-Guerrero, I. M. 2017. How Economic Freedom Affects Opportunity and Necessity Entrepreneurship in the OECD Countries. *Journal of Business Research.* 73:30–37.

Arnold, G. 2015. Street-Level Policy Entrepreneurship. *Public Management Review.* 17(3):307–327.

Arnold, G. 2021. Does Entrepreneurship Work? Understanding What Policy Entrepreneurs Do and Whether It Matters. *Policy Studies Journal.* 49(4): 968–991.

Arnold, G., Klasic, M., Wu, C., Schomburg, M., & York, A. (2023). Finding, Distinguishing, and Understanding Overlooked Policy Entrepreneurs. *Policy Sciences.* 56(4):657–687. https://doi.org/10.1007/s11077-023-09515-4.

Battilana, J., Leca, B., & Boxenbaum, E. 2009. How Actors Change Institutions: Towards a Theory of Institutional Entrepreneurship. *The Academy of Management Annals.* 3(1):65–107.

Baumgartner, F. R., & Jones, B. D. 2009. *Agendas and Insability in American Politics.* 2nd ed. Chicago: Chicago Press.

Baumgartner, F. R., Jones, B. D., & Mortensen, P. B. 2023. Punctuated Equilibrium Theory: Explaining Stabiity and Change in Public Policymaking. In Weible, C. M. (ed.). *Theories of the Policy Process* (65–99). New York: Routledge.

Beck, U. 1992. *Risk Society: Towards a New Modernity.* London: Sage.

Becker, P., Sparf, J., & Petridou, E. (2024), Identifying Proactive and Reactive Policy Entrepreneurs in Collaborative Networks in Flood Risk Management. *Policy & Politics.* 1–23.

Bernstein, D. 2023. No Changes on Horizon to Limit Gov. Inslee's Emergency Powers. News Radio 560 KPQ. March 2, 2023. https://kpq.com/no-changes-on-horizon-to-limit-gov-inslees-emergency-powers/.

Birkland, T. A. 1997. *After Disaster: Agenda Setting, Public Policy and Focusing Events*. Washington, DC: Georgetown University Press.

Birkland, T. A. 2004. Learning and Policy Improvement after Disaster: The Case of Aviation Security. *American Behavioral Scientist*. 48(3):341–364.

Birkland, T. A. 2006. *Lessons of Disaster: Policy Change after Catastrophic Events*. Washington, DC: Georgetown University Press.

Birkland, T. A. 2009. Disasters, Catastrophes, and Policy Failure in the Homeland Security Era. *Review of Policy Research*. 26(4):423–438.

Birkland, T. A., & Nath, R. 2000. Business and Political Dimensions in Disaster Management. *Journal of Public Policy*. 20(3):275–303.

Birkland, T. A., Taylor, K., Crow, D. A., & DeLeo, R. 2021. Governing in a Polarized Era: Federalism and the Response of U.S. State and Federal Governments to the COVID-19 Pandemic. *Publius: The Journal of Federalism*. 51(4):650–672.

Birkmann, J., Buckle, P., Jaeger, J., et al. 2010. Extreme Events and Disasters: A Window of Opportunity for Change? Analysis of Organizational, Institutional and Political Changes, Formal and Informal Responses after Mega-Disasters. *Natural Hazards*. 55:637–655.

Blaikie, P. M. 2009. The Tsunami of 2004 in Sri Lanka: An Introduction to Impacts and Policy in the Shadow of Civil War. *Norsk Geografisk Tidsskrift-Norwegian Journal of Geography*. 63(1):2–9.

Blavoukos, S., & Bourantonis, D. 2012. Policy Entrepreneurs and Foreign Policy Change: The Greek–Turkish Rapprochement in the 1990s. *Government & Opposition*. 47(4):597–617.

Boin, A., Ekengren, M., & Rhinard, M. 2020. Hiding in Plain Sight: Conceptualizing the Creeping Crisis. *Risk, Hazards & Crisis in Public Policy*. 11(2):116–138.

Boin, A., 't Hart, P., & McConnell, A. 2008. *Governing after Crisis : The Politics of Investigation, Accountability and Learning*. Cambridge: Cambridge University Press. http://catalog.lib.ncsu.edu/record/NCSU2126377.

Boin, A., 't Hart, P., Stern, E., & Sundelius, B. 2017. *The Politics of Crisis Management: Public Leadership under Pressure*. 2nd ed. Cambridge: Cambridge University Press.

Bothner, F., Schrader, S. M., Bandau, F., & Holzhauser, N. 2022. Never Let a Serious Crisis Go to Waste: The Introduction of Supplemental Carbon Taxes in Europe. *Journal of Public Policy*. 42(2):343–363.

Brändström, A., Kuipers, S., & Daléus, P. 2008. The Politics of Tsunami Responses: Comparing Patterns of Blame Management in Scandinavia. In Boin, A., McConnell, A., & 't Hart. P. (eds.). *Governing after Crisis: The Politics of Investigation, Accountability, and Learning* (114–147). Cambridge: Cambridge University Press.

Brecher, M., Wilkenfeld, J., & Moser, S. 1988. *Crises in the Twentieth Century: Handbook of Foreign Policy Crises*. Oxford: Pergamon Press.

Busenberg, G. J. 2001. Learning in Organizations and Public Policy. *Journal of Public Policy*. 21(2):173–189.

Cadelago, C. 2023. "We Would've Done Everything Differently": Newsom Reflects on Covid Approach. *Politico*. September 10, 2023. www.politico .com/news/2023/09/10/newsom-covid-california-00114888.

Cairney, P. 2018. Three Habits of Successful Policy Entrepreneurs. *Policy & Politics*. 46(2):199–215.

Callaghan, T., & Sylvester, S. (2021). Private Citizens as Policy Entrepreneurs: Evidence from Autism Mandates and Parental Political Mobilization. *Policy Studies Journal*. 49(1):123–145.

Capano, G., & Galanti, M. T. 2018. Policy Dynamics and Types of Agency: From Individual to Collective Patterns of Action. *European Policy Analysis*. 4(1):23–47.

Capano, G., & Galanti, M. T. 2021. From Policy Entrepreneurs to Policy Entrepreneurship: Actors and Actions in Public Policy Innovation. *Policy & Politics*. 49(3):321–342.

Capano, G., & Howlett, M. 2009. Conclusion: A Research Agenda for Policy Dynamics. In Capano, G., & Howlett, M. (eds.). *European and North American Policy Change* (1–12). New York: Routledge.

Carter, A. 2020. Yale, Harvard, Sen. Ted Kennedy: How Mandy Cohen Prepared to Handle a Pandemic in NC. Raleigh News & Observer. April 24, 2020. www .newsobserver.com/news/politics-government/article242241516.html.

Carter, R. G., & Scott, J. M. 2009. *Choosing to Lead: Understanding Congressional Foreign Policy Entrepreneurs*. Durham: Duke University Press.

Carter, R. G., & Scott, J. M. 2010. Understanding Congressional Foreign Policy Innovators: Mapping Entrepreneurs and Their Strategies. *The Social Science Journal*. 47(2):418–438.

Casson, M. 1982. *The Entrepreneur: An Economic Theory*. Totowa: Barnes and Noble.

Christensen, T., Lægreid, P., & Rykkja, L.H. 2016. Organizing for Crisis Management: Building Governance Capacity and Legitimacy. *Public Administration Review*. 76(6):887–897.

Cohen, N. 2021. *Policy Entrepreneurship at the Street Level: Understanding the Effect of the Individual*. Cambridge: Cambridge University Press.

Cohen, N., Arnold, G., & Petridou, E. 2023. Why We Need to Study Street-Level Policy Entrepreneurs. *European Policy Analysis*. 9(4):342–355.

Cohrs, R. 2021. Andrew Cuomo's Covid-19 Nursing Home Fiasco Shows the Ethical Perils of Pandemic Policymaking. *STAT* (blog). February 26, 2021. www.statnews.com/2021/02/26/cuomos-nursing-home-fiasco-ethical-perils-pandemic-policymaking/.

Colliver, V. 2021. Gavin Newsom Feared a Vaccine Nightmare: So He Outsourced California's Rollout. *Politico*. March 22, 2021. www.politico.com/states/states/california/story/2021/03/22/why-newsom-isnt-counting-on-his-own-government-to-manage-vaccine-rollout-1368548.

Congleton, R. D. 2023. Federalism and Pandemic Policies: Variety as the Spice of Life. *Public Choice*. 195(1):73–100.

Copeland, P., & James, S. 2014. Policy Windows, Ambiguity and Commission Entrepreneurship: Explaining the Relaunch of the European Union's Economic Reform Agenda. *Journal of European Public Policy*. 21(1):1–19.

Darling, J. R. 1994. Crisis Management in International Business: Key to Effective Decision-Making. *Leadership & Organization Development Journal*. 15(8):3–8.

David, C. P. 2015. Policy Entrepreneurs and the Reorientation of National Security Policy under the GW Bush Administration (2001–04). *Politics & Policy*. 43(1):163–195.

Dawsey, J., & Abutaleb, Y. 2020. "A Whole Lot of Hurt": Fauci Warns of Covid-19 Surge, Offers Blunt Assessment of Trump's Response. *Washington Post*, November 2, 2020. www.washingtonpost.com/politics/fauci-covid-winter-forecast/2020/10/31/e3970eb0-1b8b-11eb-bb35-2dcfdab0a345_story.html.

DeLeo, R. A. 2010. Anticipatory-Conjectural Policy Problems: A Case Study of Avian Influenza. *Risk Hazards & Crisis In Public Policy*. 1(1):147–184.

DeLeo, R. A. (2016). *Anticipatory Policymaking: When Government Acts to Prevent Problems and Why It Is so Difficult*. New York: Routledge.

Dias, P., Dissanayake, R., & Chandratilake, R. 2006. Lessons Learned from Tsunami Damage in Sri Lanka. *Proceedings of the Institution of Civil Engineers-Civil Engineering*. 159(2):74–81.

Doherty, B. 2021. The Patriot Act's Poisoned Tree. *Reason.Com* (blog). October 26, 2021. https://reason.com/2021/10/26/the-patriot-acts-poisoned-tree/.

Dolan, D. A. 2021. Multiple Partial Couplings in the Multiple Streams Framework: The Case of Extreme Weather and Climate Change Adaptation. *Policy Studies Journal*. 49(1):164–189.

Domanska, M. 2021. Putin's Article: "On the Historical Unity of Russians and Ukrainians." July 13. Warsaw: Centre for Eastern Studies. www.osw.waw.pl/en/o-nas.

van den Dool, A., & Li, J. 2023. What Do We Know about the Punctuated Equilibrium Theory in China? A Systematic Review and Research Priorities. *Policy Studies Journal.* 51(2):283–305.

Downs, A. 1972. Up and Down with Ecology: The Issue Attention Cycle. *The Public Interest.* 28(Summer):38–50.

Drennan, L. T., McConnell, A., & Stark, A. 2015. *Risk and Crisis Management in the Public Sector.* 2nd ed. New York: Routledge.

Dror, Y. 1993. Steering Requisites for Crises-Opportunities: On-Going Challenges. *Journal of Contingencies & Crisis Management.* 1(1):13. http://search.ebscohost.com/login.aspx?direct=true&db=buh&AN=10473500&site=ehost-live.

Dunleavy, P. 1990. Reinterpreting the Westland Affair: Theories of the State and Core Executive Decision Making. *Public Administration.* 68(1):29–60.

Eckel, M. 2023. How Did Everybody Get the Ukraine Invasion Predictions so Wrong? *Radio Free Europe/Radio Liberty.* February 17. www.rferl.org/a/russia-ukraine-invasion-predictions-wrong-intelligence/32275740.html.

Edelman, M. 1977. *Political Language: Words that Succeed and Policies that Fail.* New York: Academic Press.

Ekengren, M. 2024. Why Are We Surprised by Extreme Weather, Pandemics and Migration Crises when We Know They Will Happen? Exploring the Added Value of Contingency Thinking. *Journal of Contingencies and Crisis Management.* 32(1):e12515.

Eksborg, A.-L. 2003. Vem leder samhället i kris? [Who Leads Society during Crises?] *Kungliga Krisvetenskapsakademiens Handlingar och Tidskrift.* 6:51–64.

Ellis, W. W. 2004. Terrorism in the United States: Revisiting the Hart-Rudman Commission. *Mediterranean Quarterly.* 15(2):25–37.

Euronews. 2022. Biden Vows to Halt Russia in Ukraine: "Freedom Will Always Triumph over Tyranny." March 2. www.euronews.com/2022/03/02/biden-vows-to-halt-russia-in-ukraine-freedom-will-always-triumph-over-tyranny.

Evans, B., & Reid, J. 2014. *Resilient Life: The Art of Living Dangerously.* Malden, MA: Polity.

Faling, M., Biesbroek, R., Karlsson-Vinkhuyzen, S., & Termeer, K. 2018. Policy Entrepreneurship across Boundaries: A Systematic Literature Review. *Journal of Public Policy.* 39(2):393–422.

Featherstone, K. 2011. The Greek Sovereign Debt Crisis and EMU: A Failing State in a Skewed Regime. *Journal of Common Market Studies.* 49(2):193–217.

Ferré-Sadurní, L., & Goodman, J. D. 2021. Cuomo Resigns Amid Scandals, Ending Decade-Long Run in Disgrace. *The New York Times*. August 10, 2021. www.nytimes.com/2021/08/10/nyregion/andrew-cuomo-resigns.html.

Frisch Aviram, N., Cohen, N., & Beeri, I. 2020. Wind(ow) of Change: A Systematic Review of Policy Entrepreneurship Characteristics and Strategies. *Policy Studies Journal*. 48(3):612–644.

Fuchs, H. 2022. The Influencers behind the Ukrainian PR Machine. *Politico*. March 18. www.politico.com/news/2022/03/17/influencers-ukrainian-pr-machine-00018299.

Galan, A. 2018. The Shifting Boundaries of Legitimacy in International Law. *Nordic Journal of International Law*. 87(4):434–465.

Garrison, J. A. 2017. Small Group Effects on Foreign Policy Decision-Making. In Harnish, S., Kaarbo, J., & Oppermann, K. (eds.). *The Oxford Encyclopedia of Foreign Policy Analysis*. Oxford: Oxford University Press.

Garsten, C., Rothstein, B., & Svallfors, S. 2022. *Makt utan mandat : de policy-professionella i svensk politik*. Stockholm: Dialogos.

Gasulla, Ó., Bel, G., & Mazaira-Font, F. A. 2023. Ideology, Political Polarisation and Agility of Policy Responses: Was Weak Executive Federalism a Curse or a Blessing for COVID-19 Management in the USA? *Cambridge Journal of Regions, Economy and Society*. 16(1):151–166.

Gostin, L. O., Friedman, E. A., & Wetter, S. A. 2020. Responding to Covid-19: How to Navigate a Public Health Emergency Legally and Ethically. *Hastings Center Report*. 50(2), 8–12.

Gotham, K. F., & Greenberg, M. 2014. *Crisis Cities: Disaster and Redevelopment in New York and New Orleans*. Oxford: Oxford University Press.

Hand, M. C., Morris, M., & Rai, V. 2023. The Role of Policy Narrators during Crisis: A Micro-Level Analysis of the Sourcing, Synthesizing, and Sharing of Policy Narratives in Rural Texas. *Policy Studies Journal*. 51:843–868.

Hansén, D. 2005. Den svenska hanteringen av tsunamikatastrofen: fokus på Regeringskansliet [The Swedish Management of the Tsunami Disaster: Focus on the Government Offices]. In SOU *Sverige och tsunamin: Katastrofkommissions rappott. Expert rapporter från 2005 års katastrof-kommission [Sweden and the Tsunami: The Report of the Disaster Commission Expert Reports from the 2005 Disaster Commission]*. Government Offices of Sweden. SOU 2205:104.

't Hart, P. 1993. Symbols, Rituals and Power: The Lost Dimensions of Crisis Management. *Journal of Contingencies and Crisis Management*. 1(1):36–50.

't Hart, P., & Boin, A. 2001. Between Crisis and Normalcy: The Long Shadow of Post-Crisis Politics. In Rosenthal, U., Boin, A., & Comfort, L. K. (eds.).

Managing Crises: Threats, Dilemmas, Opportunities (28–48). Springfield: Charles C Thomas.

Hay, C. 2007. *Why We Hate Politics*. Cambridge: Polity.

Herweg, N., Huß, C., & Zohlnhöfer, R. 2015. Straightening the Three Streams: Theorising Extensions of the Multiple Streams Framework. *European Journal of Political Research*. 54(3):435–449.

Herweg, N., Zahariadis, N., & Zohlnhöfer, R. 2023. The Multiple Streams Framework: Foundations, Refinements, and Empirical Applications. In Weible, C (ed.). *Theories of the Policy Process* (29–64). New York: Routledge.

Hjorth, D. 2003. *Rewriting Entrepreneurship: For a New Perspective on Organisational Creativity*. Stockholm: Liber.

Hood, C. 2011. *The Blame Game: Spin, Bureaucracy, and Self-Preservation in Government*. Princeton: Princeton University Press.

Huq, A. 2020. Perspective | States Can Band Together to Fight the Virus – No Matter What Trump Does. *Washington Post*, April 17. www.washingtonpost .com/outlook/2020/04/15/states-coronavirus-agreements-reopen/.

Ingold, K. 2011. Network Structures within Policy Processes: Coalitions, Power, and Brokerage in Swiss Climate Policy. *Policy Studies Journal*. 39(3):435–459.

IPCC. 2023. *Climate Change 2023: Synthesis Report. Contribution of Working Groups I, II and III to the Sixth Assessment Report of the Intergovernmental Panel on Climate Change* [Core Writing Team, H. Lee & J. Romero (eds.)]. IPCC, Geneva, Switzerland, pp. 1–34, https://doi.org/10.59327/IPCC/ AR6-9789291691647.001.

Jayasuriya, S., Steele, P., & Weerakoon, D. 2006. *Post-Tsunami Recovery: Issues and Challenges in Sri Lanka*. Asian Development Bank Institute (ADBI) Research Paper Series No. 71.

Jones, M. D., Smith-Walter, A., Mc Beth, M., & Shanahan, E. A. 2023. The Narrative Policy Framework. In Weible, C. M. (ed.). *Theories of the Policy Process*(161–195). New York: Routledge.

Jost, K. 2004. *Re-examining 9/11*. Thousand Oaks: CQ Press.

Kapucu, N., & Hu, Q. 2022. An Old Puzzle and Unprecedented Challenges: Coordination in Response to the COVID-19 Pandemic in the US. *Public Performance & Management Review*. 45(4):773–798.

Kettl, D. F. 2020. States Divided: The Implications of American Federalism for COVID-19. *Public Administration Review*. 80(4):595–602.

Kingdon, J. W. 2011. *Agendas, Alternatives, and Public Policies*. 2nd ed. New York: Pearson.

Kirzner, I. M. 1973. *Competition and Entrepreneurship*. Chicago: University of Chicago Press.

Kirzner, I. M. 1997. Entrepreneurial Discovery and the Competitive Market Process: An Austrian Approach. *Journal of Economic Literature.* 35(1):60–85.

Kolie, D., Delamou, A., van de Pas, R., et al. 2019. "Never Let a Crisis Go to Waste": Post-Ebola Agenda-Setting for Health System Strengthening in Guinea. *BMJ Global Health.* 4(6):e001925.

Konisky, D. M., & Nolette, P. 2021. The State of American Federalism, 2020–2021: Deepening Partisanship amid Tumultuous Times. *Publius: The Journal of Federalism.* 51(3):327–364.

Larsson, T., & Bäck, H. 2008. *Governing and Governance in Sweden.* Malmö: Studentlitteratur.

Lawrence, R. G., & Birkland, T. A. 2004. Guns, Hollywood, and Criminal Justice: Defining the School Shootings Problem across Public Arenas. *Social Science Quarterly.* 85(5):1193–1207.

Levy, J. S. 2008. Case Studies: Types, Designs, and Logics of Inference. *Conflict Management and Peace Science.* 25(1):1–18.

Lewis, E. 1980. *Public Entrepreneurship: Towards a Theory of Bureaucratic Power.* Bloomington: Indiana University Press.

Maitlis, S., & Sonenshein, S. 2010. Sensemaking in Crisis and Change: Inspiration and Insights from Weick (1988). *Journal of Management Studies.* 47(3):551–580.

May, P. J. 1991. Reconsidering Policy Design: Policies and Publics. *Journal of Public Policy.* 11(2):187–206.

May, P. J. 1992. Policy Learning and Failure. *Journal of Public Policy.* 12(4):331–354.

McBeth, M. K., & Shanahan, E. A. 2004. Public Opinion for Sale: The Role of Policy Marketers in Greater Yellowstone Policy Conflict. *Policy Sciences.* 37(3):319–338.

McCaffrey, M., & Salerno, J. T. 2011. A Theory of Political Entrepreneurship. *Modern Economy.* 2(4):552–560.

McConnell, A. 2003. Overview: Crisis Management, Influences, Responses and Evaluation. *Parliamentary Affairs.* 56(3):363–409.

Meydani, A. 2015. Political Entrepreneurs and Institutional Change: Governability, Liberal Political Culture, and the 1992 Electoral Reform in Israel. In Narbutaité Aflaki, I., Petridou, E., & Miles, L. (eds.). *Entrepreneurship in the Polis: Understanding Political Entrepreneurship* (87–102). Burlington: Ashgate.

Mintrom, M. 2000. *Policy Entrepreneurs and School Choice.* Washington, DC: Georgetown University Press.

Mintrom, M. 2019a. *Policy Entrepreneurs and Dynamic Change.* Cambridge: Cambridge University Press.

Mintrom, M. 2019b. So You Want to Be a Policy Entrepreneur? *Policy Design and Practice.* 2(4):307–323.

Mintrom, M., & Norman, P. 2009. Policy Entrepreneurship and Policy Change. *Policy Studies Journal.* 37(4):649–667.

Mitra, J. (2012). *Entrepreneurship, Innovation and Regional Development: An Introduction.* New York: Routledge.

Mitra, J. (2009). Learning to Grow: How New, Small, High Technology Firms Acquire Cognitive and Socio-political Legitimacy in their Regions. *International Journal of Technology Management.* 46(3–4):344–370.

MSB (Swedish Civil Contingencies Agency). 2016. Ansvar, samverkan, handling. Åtgärder för stärkt krisberedskap utifrån erfarenheterna från skogsbranden i Västmanland 2014. [Responsibility, Collaboration, Action. Measures towards Strengthened Crisis Management Based on Lessons from the Forest Fire in Västmanland 2014]. Karlstad: MSB.

The National Commission on Terrorist Attacks Upon the United States. 2004. https://9-11commission.gov/report/.

NBC News Chicago. 2020. Midwest Governors Announce Plan to Coordinate on Reopening of Economy. NBC Chicago. April 16. www.nbcchicago.com/news/coronavirus/midwest-governors-announce-plan-to-coordinate-on-reopening-of-economy/2256936/.

Neelon, B., Mutiso, F., Mueller, N. T., Pearce, J. L., & Benjamin-Neelon, S. E. 2021. Associations between Governor Political Affiliation and COVID-19 Cases, Deaths, and Testing in the U.S. *American Journal of Preventive Medicine.* 61(1):115–119.

Nehamas, N., & LaFraniere, S. 2023. DeSantis Leans into Vaccine Skepticism to Energize Struggling Campaign. *The New York Times,* November 2. www.nytimes.com/2023/11/02/us/politics/desantis-covid.html.

Nohrstedt, D., Ingold, K., Weible, C. M., et al. 2023. The Advocacy Coalition Framework: Progress and Emerging Areas. In Weible, C. M. (ed.). *Theories of the Policy Process* (130–160). New York: Routledge.

Nohrstedt, D., & Weible, C. M. 2010. The Logic of Policy Change after Crisis: Proximity and Subsystem Interaction. *Risk, Hazards & Crisis in Public Policy.* 1(2):1–32.

Nowlin, M. C. 2011. Theories of the Policy Process: State of the Research and Emerging Trends. *Policy Studies Journal.* 39:41–60.

Nygaard-Christensen, M., & Houborg, E. 2023. Pandemic Lockdown as Policy Window for Street-Level Innovation of Health and Substitution Treatment Services for People Who Use Drugs. *Drugs, Habits and Social Policy.* 24(3):232–245.

Office of Governor Gavin Newsom. 2021. Governor Newsom Issues 2021 Social Innovation Impact Report Supporting Efforts to Tackle the State's Most Persistent Challenges. California Governor. December 13. www.gov.ca.gov/2021/12/13/governor-newsom-issues-2021-social-innovation-impact-report-supporting-efforts-to-tackle-the-states-most-persistent-challenges/.

Office of Governor Ron DeSantis. 2023. Governor Ron DeSantis Announces Initiative to Make Protections from COVID Mandates Permanent, Enact New Protections for Free Speech for Medical Practitioners. January 17. www.flgov.com/2023/01/17/governor-ron-desantis-announces-initiative-to-make-protections-from-covid-mandates-permanent-enact-new-protections-for-free-speech-for-medical-practitioners/.

Oprysko, C. 2022. What PR Firms Are Doing for Ukraine's Ministry of Culture. *Politico*. August 26. www.politico.com/newsletters/politico-influence/2022/08/26/what-pr-firms-are-doing-for-ukraines-ministry-of-culture-00053979.

Ostrom, E. (2005). *Unlocking Public Entrepreneurship and Public Economies*. WIDER Discussion Paper No. 2005/01.

Park, A. 2022. Dr. Anthony Fauci Is Stepping Down. Here's His Advice for His Successor. *Time*. December 20. https://time.com/6242342/dr-anthony-fauci-stepping-down/.

Parker, C. F., & Dekker, S. 2008. September 11 and Postcrisis Investigation: Exploring the Role and Impact of the 9/11 Commission. In Boin, A., McConnell, A., & 't hart, P. (eds.). *Governing after Crisis* (255–282). Cambridge: Cambridge University Press.

Parker, C. F., & Stern, E. K. 2022. The Trump Administration and the COVID-19 Crisis: Exploring the Warning-Response Problems and Missed Opportunities of a Public Health Emergency. *Public Administration*. 100(3):616–632.

Perrow, C. 1999. *Normal Accidents: Living with High Risk Technologies*. Princeton: Princeton University Press.

Peters, B. G., & Pierre, J. 2004. Politicization of the Civil Service: Concepts, Causes, Consequences. In Peters, B. G., & Pierre, J. (eds.). *Politicization of the Civil Service in Comparative Perspective: The Quest for Control*. Routledge.

Peters, B. G., & Pierre, J. 2022. Politicisation of the Public Service during Democratic Backsliding: Alternative Perspectives. *Australian Journal of Public Administration*. 81(4):629–639.

Petridou, E. 2014. Theories of the Policy Process: Contemporary Scholarship and Future Directions. *Policy Studies Journal*. 42:S12–S32.

Petridou, E. 2017. *Political Entrepreneurship in Swedish: Towards a (Re)theorization of Entrepreneurial Agency*. Doctoral Dissertation. Sundsvall: Mid Sweden University.

Petridou, E. 2020. Politics and Administration in Times of Crisis: Explaining the Swedish Response to the COVID-19 Crisis. *European Policy Analysis.* 6(2):147–158.

Petridou, E. 2023. From Policy Entrepreneur to Policy Entrepreneurship: Examining the Role of Context in Policy Entrepreneurial Action. In Zahariadis, N., Herweg, N., Zohlnhöfer, R., & Petridou, E. (eds.). *A Modern Guide to the Multiple Streams Framework.* (104–119) New York: Routledge.

Petridou, E., Johansson, R., Eriksson, K., Alirani, G., & Zahariadis, N. 2024. Theorizing Reactive Policy Entrepreneurship: A Case Study of Swedish Local Emergency Management. *Policy Studies Journal.* 52(1):73–89.

Petridou, E., & Mintrom, M. 2021. A Research Agenda for the Study of Policy Entrepreneurs. *Policy Studies Journal.* 49(4):943–967.

Petridou, E., Narbutaité Aflaki, I., & Miles, L. 2015. Unpacking the Theoretical Boxes of Political Entrepreneurship. In Narbutaité Aflaki, I., Petridou, E., & Miles, L. (eds.). *Entrepreneurship in the Polis: Understanding Political Entrepreneurship* (1–16). Burlington, VT: Ashgate.

Petridou, E., & Sparf, J. 2017. For Safety's Sake: The Strategies of Institutional Entrepreneurs and Bureaucratic Reforms in Swedish Crisis Management, 2001–2009. *Policy and Society.* 36(4):556–574.

Pralle, S. B. 2003. Venue Shopping, Political Strategy, and Policy Change: The Internationalization of Canadian Forest Advocacy. *Journal of Public Policy.* 23(3):233–260.

Radin, B. A. 2013. *Beyond Machiavelli: Policy Analysis Reaches Midlife.* 2nd ed. Washington, DC: Georgetown University Press.

Rainbird, J. S. 1976. *The Vigiles of Rome.* Doctoral thesis, Durham University.

Reynolds, P. D., Bygrave, W. D., Autio, E., Cox, L. W., & Hay, M. 2002. *Global Entrepreneurship Monitor: 2002 Executive Report.* Kauffman Foundation.

Roberts, N. C., & King, P. J. 1991. Policy Entrepreneurs: Their Activity Structure and Function in the Policy Process. *Journal of Public Administration Research and Theory.* 1(2):147–175.

Rosenthal, U., Charles, M. T., & Hart, P. T. (eds.). 1989. *Coping with Crises: The Management of Disasters, Riots, and Terrorism.* Springfield: Charles C. Thomas.

Rosenthal, U., & Kouzmin, A. 1997. Crises and Crisis Management: Toward Comprehensive Government Decision-Making. *Journal of Public Administration Research and Theory.* 7(2):277–304.

Rubin, C. B., Cumming, W. B., Tanali, I. R., & Birkland, T. A. 2003. Major Terrorism Events and Their US Outcomes (1988–2001). Natural Hazards Research Working Paper #107. Boulder: Natural Hazards Research and Applications Information Center, Institute of Behavioral Science, University of Colorado. www.colorado.edu/hazards/wp/wp107/wp107.html.

Rubin, O., Errett, N. A., Upshur, R., & Baekkeskov, E. 2021. The Challenges Facing Evidence-Based Decision-Making in the Initial Response to COVID-19. *Scandinavian Journal of Public Health*. 49(7):790–796.

Sakalasuriya, M., Haigh, R., Hettige, S., et al. 2020. Governance, Institutions and People within the Interface of a Tsunami Early Warning System. *Politics and Governance*. 8(4):432–444.

Sarkissian, A. 2023. Florida Surgeon General Altered Key Findings in Study on Covid-19 Vaccine Safety. *Politico*. April 24. www.politico.com/news/2023/04/24/florida-surgeon-general-covid-vaccine-00093510.

Saurugger, S., & Terpan, F. 2016. Do Crises Lead to Policy Change? The Multiple Streams Framework and the European Union's Economic Governance Instruments. *Policy Sciences*. 49:35–53.

Schattschneider, E. E. 1975. *The Semisovereign People*. Hinsdale: The Dryden Press.

Schmitt, M. N. 2022. Russia's "Special Military Operation" and Its (Claimed) Right of Self-Defense. February 28. Lieber Institute. https://lieber.westpoint.edu/russia-special-military-operation-claimed-right-self-defense/.

Schneider, M., & Teske, P. 1992. Toward a Theory of the Political Entrepreneur: Evidence from Local Government. *The American Political Science Review*. 86(3):737–747.

Schneider, M., Teske, P., & Mintrom, M. 1995. *Public Entrepreneurs: Agents of Change in American Government*. Princeton: Princeton University Press.

Seeger, M. W., Sellnow, T. L., & Ulmer, R. R. 1998. Communication, Organization, and Crisis. *Annals of the International Communication Association*. 21(1):231–276.

Shaluf, I. M., Ahmadun, F. L. R., & Mat Said, A. 2003. A Review of Disaster and Crisis. *Disaster Prevention and Management: An International Journal*. 12(1):24–32.

SOU. 2005. *Sverige och tsunamin: Katastrofkommissions rapport [Sweden and the Tsunami: The Report of the Disaster Commission]*. Government Offices of Sweden. SOU 2205:104.

SOU. 2018. *En effektivare kommunal räddningstjänst [More Effective Municipal Rescue Services]*. Government Offices of Sweden. SOU 2018:54.

SOU. 2019. *Skogsbränderna sommaren 2018 [The Forest Fires in the Summer of 2018]*. Government Offices of Sweden. SOU 2019:7.

Spill, R. L., Licari, M. J., & Ray, L. 2001. Taking on Tobacco: Policy Entrepreneurship and the Tobacco Litigation. *Political Research Quarterly*. 54(3):605–622.

Stern, E. 1997. Crisis and Learning: A Conceptual Balance Sheet. *Journal of Contingencies and Crisis Management*. 5(2):69–86.

Stillman II, R. J. 2005. *Public Administration: Concepts and Cases.* 8th ed. Boston: Houghton Mifflin.

Stivers, C. 2022. Public Service in the Pandemic Era: A COVID Commentary. *Public Administration Review.* 82(2):354–358.

Stone, D. A. 2002. *Policy Paradox: The Art of Political Decision Making.* New York: WW Norton.

Stranks, J. 1994. *Human Factors and Safety.* London: Pitman.

Svensson, P. 2019. Formalized Policy Entrepreneurship as a Governance Tool for Policy Integration. *International Journal of Public Administration.* 42(14):1212–1221.

Taylor, K., DeLeo, R. A., Albright, E., et al. 2023. Estimating the Effect of Policy Entrepreneurship on Individual Vaccination Behavior during the COVID-19 Pandemic. *European Policy Analysis.* ep 2.1198. https://doi.org/10.1002/epa2.1198.

Taylor, K., DeLeo, R. A., Crow, D. A., & Birkland, T. A. 2022. The US Response to the COVID-19 Pandemic: Incoherent Leadership, Fractured Federalism, and Squandered Capacity. In Zahariadis, N., Petridou, E., Exadaktylos, T., & Sparf, J. (eds.). *Policy Styles and Trust in the Age of Pandemics: Global Threat, National Responses* (191–208). London: Routledge.

Theodossopoulos, D. 2013. Infuriated with the Infuriated? Blaming Tactics and Discontent about the Greek Financial Crisis. *Current Anthropology.* 54(2): 200–221.

Tierney, K. 2005. The 9/11 Commission and Disaster Management: Little Depth, Less Context, Not Much Guidance. *Contemporary Sociology.* 34(2): 115–120.

Timmermans, J., van der Heiden, S., & Born, M. P. 2014. Policy Entrepreneurs in Sustainability Transitions: Their Personality and Leadership Profiles Assessed. *Environmental Innovation and Societal Transitions.* 13:96–108.

Tsebelis, G. 2015. Lessons from the Greek Crisis. *Journal of European Public Policy.* 23(1):1–17.

UNESCO. 2019. *Tsunami Warning and Mitigation Systems to Protect Coastal Communities.* https://unesdoc.unesco.org/ark:/48223/pf0000373791.

Van Beek, M. 2020. Michigan Supreme Court Upholds Separation of Powers. Mackinac Center. October 12. www.mackinac.org/michigan-supreme-court-upholds-separation-of-powers.

Verduijn, S. 2015. Setting the Political Agenda: A Policy Entrepreneurial Perspective on Urban Development in the Netherlands. In Narbutaité Aflaki, I., Petridou, E., & Miles, L. (eds.). *Entrepreneurship in the Polis: Understanding Political Entrepreneurship* (55–72). Burlington, VT: Ashgate.

Villegas, P. 2020. Trump Says He Might Fire Fauci: Technically, He Can't. *Washington Post*, November 2. www.washingtonpost.com/health/2020/11/02/can-trump-fire-fauci/.

Vince, J. 2023. A Creeping Crisis when an Urgent Crisis Arises: The Reprioritization of Plastic Pollution Issues during COVID-19. *Politics & Policy.* 51(1):26–40.

Weick, K. 1995. *Sensemaking in Organizations*. London: Sage.

Weir, F. 2022. Russia Says It's Fighting Nazis in Ukraine: It Doesn't Mean What You Think. *Christian Science Monitor*. April 20. www.csmonitor.com/World/Europe/2022/0420/Russia-says-it-s-fighting-Nazis-in-Ukraine.-It-doesn-t-mean-what-you-think.

Weissert, C. S., Uttermark, M. J., Mackie, K. R., & Artiles, A. 2021. Governors in Control: Executive Orders, State-Local Preemption, and the COVID-19 Pandemic. *Publius.* 51(3):396–428.

Wenzelburger, G., König, P. D., & Wolf, F. 2019. Policy Theories in Hard Times? Assessing the Explanatory Power of Policy Theories in the Context of Crisis. *Public Organization Review.* 19:97–118.

Wilson, W. 1887. The Study of Administration. *Political Science Quarterly.* 2 (June):197–222.

Zahariadis, N. 2003. *Ambiguity and Choice in Public Policy: Political Decision-Making in Modern Democracies*. Washington, DC: Georgetown Press.

Zahariadis, N. 2010. Greece's Debt Crisis: A National Tragedy of European Proportions. *Mediterranean Quarterly.* 21(4):34–58.

Zahariadis, N. 2013. Complexity, Coupling and Policy Effectiveness: The European Response to the Greek Sovereign Debt Crisis. *Journal of Public Policy.* 32(2):99–116.

Zahariadis, N. 2016. Values as Barriers to Compromise? Ideology, Transnational Coalitions, and Distributive Bargaining in Negotiations over the Third Greek Bailout. *International Negotiation.* 21(3):473–494.

Zahariadis, N. 2007. The Multiple Streams Framework: Structure, Limitations, Prospects. In Sabatier, P.A. (ed.). *Theories of the Policy Process*. Boulder, CO: Westview.

Zahariadis, N., & Exadaktylos, T. 2016. Policies that Succeed and Programs that Fail: Ambiguity, Conflict, and Crisis in Greek Higher Education. *Policy Studies Journal.* 44(1):59–82.

Zahariadis, N., Ceccoli, S., & Petridou, E. 2021. Assessing the Effects of Calculated Inaction on National Responses to the COVID-19 Crisis. *Risk, Hazards & Crisis in Public Policy.* 12(3):328–345.

Zahariadis, N., Herweg, N., Zohlnhöfer, R., Petridou, E., & Novotný, V. 2023. Advancing the Multiple Streams Framework. In Zahariadis, N., Herweg, N., Zohlnhöfer, R., & Petridou, E. (eds.). *A Modern Guide to Multiple Streams Framework*. Cheltenham: Edward Elgar.

Van der Zwan, P., Thurik, R., Verheul, I., & Hessels, J. 2016. Factors Influencing the Entrepreneurial Engagement of Opportunity and Necessity Entrepreneurs. *Eurasian Business Review*. 6:273–295.

"Crisis reveals character, right?"
Ethan Hawk
Interview with NPR December 8, 2023

Cambridge Elements ☰

Public Policy

M. Ramesh

National University of Singapore (NUS)

M. Ramesh is UNESCO Chair on Social Policy Design at the Lee Kuan Yew School of Public Policy, NUS. His research focuses on governance and social policy in East and Southeast Asia, in addition to public policy institutions and processes. He has published extensively in reputed international journals. He is co-editor of *Policy and Society* and *Policy Design and Practice*.

Michael Howlett

Simon Fraser University, British Columbia

Michael Howlett is Burnaby Mountain Professor and Canada Research Chair (Tier1) in the Department of Political Science, Simon Fraser University. He specialises in public policy analysis, and resource and environmental policy. He is currently editor-in-chief of *Policy Sciences* and co-editor of the *Journal of Comparative Policy Analysis, Policy and Society* and *Policy Design and Practice*.

Xun WU

Hong Kong University of Science and Technology (Guangzhou)

Xun WU is currently a Professor at the Innovation, Policy and Entrepreneurship Thrust at the Society Hub of Hong Kong University of Science and Technology (Guangzhou). He is a policy scientist with a strong interest in the linkage between policy analysis and public management. Trained in engineering, economics, public administration, and policy analysis, his research seeks to make contribution to the design of effective public policies in dealing emerging policy challenges across Asian countries.

Judith Clifton

University of Cantabria

Judith Clifton is Professor of Economics at the University of Cantabria, Spain, and Editor-in-Chief of *Journal of Economic Policy Reform*. Her research interests include the determinants and consequences of public policy across a wide range of public services, from infrastructure to health, particularly in Europe and Latin America, as well as public banks, especially, the European Investment Bank. Most recently, she is principal investigator on the Horizon Europe Project GREENPATHS (www.greenpaths.info) on the just green transition.

Eduardo Araral

National University of Singapore (NUS)

Eduardo Araral specializes in the study of the causes and consequences of institutions for collective action and the governance of the commons. He is widely published in various journals and books and has presented in more than ninety conferences. Ed was a 2021–22 Fellow at the Center for Advanced Study of Behavioral Sciences, Stanford University. He has received more than US$6.6 million in external research grants as the lead or co-PI for public agencies and corporations. He currently serves as a Special Issue Editor (collective action, commons, institutions, governance) for World Development and is a member of the editorial boards of *Water Economics and Policy, World Development Sustainability, Water Alternatives* and the *International Journal of the Commons*.

About the Series

Elements in Public Policy is a concise and authoritative collection of assessments of the state of the art and future research directions in public policy research, as well as substantive new research on key topics. Edited by leading scholars in the field, the series is an ideal medium for reflecting on and advancing the understanding of critical issues in the public sphere. Collectively, the series provides a forum for broad and diverse coverage of all major topics in the field while integrating different disciplinary and methodological approaches.

Cambridge Elements $\equiv$

Public Policy

Elements in the Series

Printed in the United States
by Baker & Taylor Publisher Services